Coexisting with URBAN WILDLIFE

A guide to the Central Arizona Uplands

ROBERT L. HOFFA

Illustrations by
Walt Anderson

Sharlot Hall Museum Press
Prescott, Arizona

© 1996
Game and Fish Department
State of Arizona
All rights reserved.
Printed in the United States of America

Sharlot Hall Museum Press
Sharlot Hall Historical Society
415 W. Gurley St.
Prescott, Arizona 86301

ISBN: 0-927579-07-3

Library of Congress Catalogue No. 95-69522

Designed and typeset by Janet Lovelady

First Edition

Acknowledgments

I would like to thank Carl Tomoff, Tom Fleischner, Harley Shaw, Walt Anderson, Dan Taylor, Rob Hunt, and all the other dedicated naturalists of the central Arizona uplands, who have helped me to observe and interpret the workings of nature.

For their technical contribution to the composition and content of this work, I would like to thank Warren Miller and Norm Tessman of Sharlot Hall Museum, Carolyn Engle-Wilson and Jim Witham of the Arizona Game and Fish Department, and Walt Anderson of Prescott College. Thanks also to Sharlot Hall Museum graphic artist George Fuller, who contributed the technical drawings on pages 3, 14, 20, 31, 37, 38, 44, 47 and 69, and to Janet Lovelady, who designed and typeset the book.

Lastly, I would like to thank Annabelle Nelson for her unwavering support, encouragement, and technical assistance throughout this project.

Research, preparation, and publication costs associated with this book have been underwritten by a generous grant from the Heritage Fund, Arizona Game and Fish Department.

*To Sage
and the other children growing
up in the central Arizona uplands.
May your generation realize the
dream of a world where the
nonhuman residents have a voice
in how we use the land.*

Contents

INTRODUCTION 1
   Habitat 4
   Attracting & Encouraging 12
   Managing Conflict 18

BACKYARD MAMMALS 25
   Bats 27
   Cottontail 33
   Rock Squirrel 36
   Abert's Squirrel 39
   Pocket Gopher 42
   Beaver 45
   Woodrat 48
   Coyote 51
   Gray Fox 54
   Raccoon 56
   Ringtail 59
   Striped Skunk 61
   Javelina 65
   Mule Deer 71
   Pronghorn 74

BACKYARD BIRDS 77
   American Kestrel 79
   Gambel's Quail 81
   Mourning Dove 83
   Barn Owl 85
   Hummingbirds 87
   Northern Flicker 89

Acorn Woodpecker	91
Scrub Jay	93
Common Raven	95
American Robin	97
European Starling	99
House Finch	101
House Sparrow	103

BACKYARD REPTILES 105
- Lizards 107
- Arizona Mountain Kingsnake 110
- Garter Snake 112
- Arizona Black Rattlesnake 114

Appendix A - Organizations & Agencies 119
Appendix B - Further Reading 121
Author and Illustrator Biographies 123

Introduction

Conserving wildlife populations begins in the heart. Watching a herd of antelope glide across the land, or admiring the agile gait of a gray fox as it slips from view, reaffirms our personal connectedness to nature. We are inspired to learn more about the animals around us. Wildlife has always been abundant in the central Arizona uplands; it is still common to view wild animals throughout the region, whether in the forests and grasslands, or in our own backyards.

The central Arizona uplands are a place of unique beauty, where the deserts give way to rolling hills and green mountains, where a diverse landscape hosts broad valleys, rivers, streams, canyons, mountains, and mesas. This panorama of natural beauty is threatened by the skyrocketing growth in human population. When people choose to live near wildness, they inevitably disturb it. The most recent census shows that from 1980 to 1990 the communities in this area grew an average of 54%. Prescott Valley grew in excess of 250%. This phenomenal rate of growth is causing tragic consequences for wildlife and wildlife habitat.

The occasional wildlife encounter encourages us to learn more about animals' behaviors and their habitats. The information in this book will help residents understand the unique roles that animals play in natural and urban environments. Perhaps along the way it will foster appreciation for the inherent value of our rich biological heritage.

In addition to being a guide to urban wildlife, this book serves as a resource for wildlife protection. Many homes and neighborhoods in central Arizona are designed to emphasize the natural setting. Yet unless we learn to coexist responsibly with wildlife, our homes endanger theirs.

A third purpose of this book is to provide assistance in managing wildlife conflicts. Not all interactions with wildlife are positive. Woodpeckers, javelina and skunks can become serious nuisances and cause expensive damage to homes and yards. *Coexisting with Urban Wildlife* offers some practical solutions. We need to remember that we are in any wild animal's backyard as much as it is in ours. There are very few wildlife problems that are not the result of people problems. Undisturbed wildlife habitat is in some ways analogous to the gardens and landscaping that people value and labor over. A hundred years ago, the areas where we live were beautiful, natural gardens rich with wildlife. The natural land is like a wildlife garden where animals make a living by finding food and shelter. When conflict with wildlife occurs, keep in mind that by moving into wildlife habitat we dug up their gardens first.

With this new awareness of our shared habitat, we can expand our perceptions to include wildlife as residents of our neighborhood. We become coinhabitants, living together, tolerating each other and accepting each other's presence.

Throughout the book, references are made to urban wildlife. This term is a generalization and refers to animals that live in cities, suburbs, towns and developing rural areas. In the central Arizona uplands, the larger urban populations are centered around Prescott, Payson, Williams and the Verde Valley. Most population centers in central Arizona are found in the middle-elevation range of the state. For this reason, the book is specific to animals and their habitats found between the elevations of 4,000 and 7,000 feet.

The bird, mammal and reptile species included in the book are those commonly found in urban environments around central Arizona. There are many other animals that

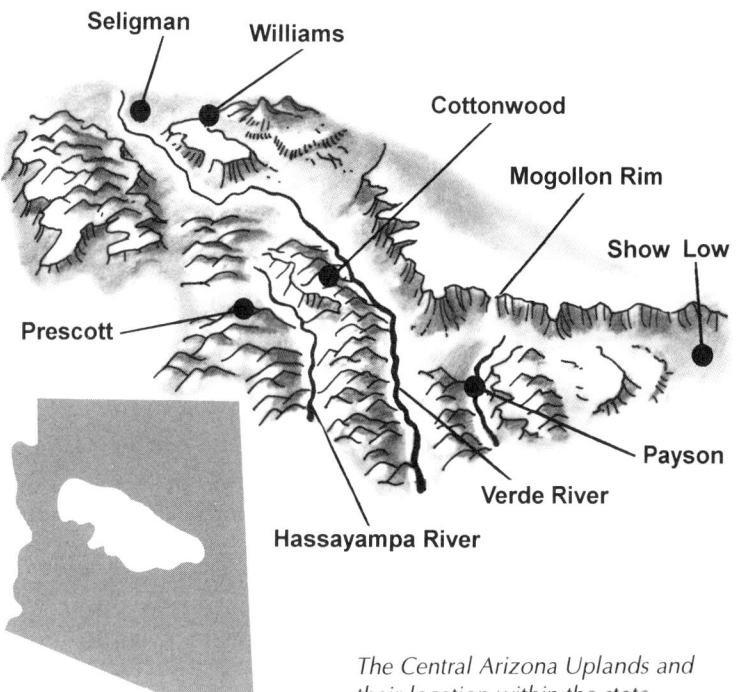

The Central Arizona Uplands and their location within the state.

can be found within urban areas or along their edges, but they are less common, and therefore not included in the scope of this book. The narrative for each species offers the reader a glimpse into the daily life of the animal, encourages positive wildlife/human interactions and gives information to help resolve nuisance-wildlife problems. The book is not intended to be a comprehensive field guide to the identification of wildlife. There are many field guides of this sort available, and this book does not attempt to duplicate previous work. Titles of books for further reference can be found in Appendix B.

Learning to coexist with our wildlife neighbors makes us better stewards of the land. It helps us understand the role that we play in the complexity of nature. We can protect our wildlife heritage *and* maintain our own quality of life in this rapidly developing region.

Habitat

Habitat is where an animal lives. It is where each species finds food, water, cover, space and a place to reproduce that matches its individual needs. The availability of these requirements is what makes up good wildlife habitat for each type of animal and determines where it will live. Animals live where they can find the types of plants and/or animals that they have evolved to eat. They choose areas where they can find the right physical features such as dense vegetation, open spaces, and soft soils or rocky crevices that provide for their shelter needs. Temperature, surface water, rainfall and other climatic conditions can also be factors that determine suitable habitat for an animal. Together these factors make up a set of life requirements that we call an animal's habitat.

An important determinant of wildlife habitat is the type of vegetation present. Trees and shrubs provide cover, food and nest sites for wildlife, and many animals live among the branches and foliage of vegetation. Some animals require open spaces so that they can see predators from a distance, while others prefer dense cover for hiding. Animals also find food in trees and shrubs. Birds glean insects from branches and leaves of trees and shrubs, and squirrels build nests among the limbs. Many animals eat the fruits and seeds that plants produce. Holes, hollows and crevices in dead trees provide homes for bats, woodpeckers and other small birds. Dead trees also create hunting perches for hawks and owls. Decaying plant material gives nutrients to the soil and is home to fungi, earthworms, millipedes and many types of insects that are part of the food chain.

Plants and animals and their interactions are sometimes called a biotic community. When we view animals as part of a biotic community, connections, patterns, and relationships begin to appear. Only then can we begin to understand the important role that every creature plays in nature.

In this book, animals are referenced to their habitats by the dominant type of vegetation found there, and by the geographic characteristics of the terrain that they prefer. The populated areas of the central Arizona uplands have five easily identified vegetation types. These are grassland, chaparral, pinyon/juniper woodland, ponderosa pine forest, and riparian. Although vegetation type is only one of many factors that determine an animal's habitat, it is a good indicator of where an animal may live. The following section describes these five vegetation types.

Grasslands: *Grasslands occur at elevations of 3,500 to 5,500 feet. They are natural open areas, dominated by a mixture of short to medium perennial and annual grasses. Grasslands can form large expanses of open fields or be broken by a scattering of shrubs or trees.*

Chaparral: Chaparral can be found from 3,500 to 6,000 feet in elevation. Chaparral refers to dense stands of shrubs made up of a mixture of species. Some of the more common shrubs that make up the chaparral complex include scrub oak, mountain mahogany, and manzanita. Central Arizona has some of the most extensive areas of chaparral in the southwestern United States.

Pinyon/juniper Woodland: *Open woodlands of pinyon and juniper trees are found at elevations of 5,000 to 6,500 feet. Pinyon/juniper woodlands vary in the dominance of tree species from equally mixed stands of pinyon and juniper to stands dominated by either species. There is often a variety of shrubs mixed within the pinyon/juniper woodlands.*

Ponderosa Pine Forest: *The ponderosa pine forest is the dominant vegetation of the higher elevations of central Arizona. It can be found from 5,000 to 7,000 feet or higher. Ponderosa pine forests vary from an open scattering of trees to a dense stand with a closed canopy of foliage overhead. An important component of the ponderosa pine vegetation type is the presence of smaller trees and shrubs that grow within the forest. Some of these species of trees and shrubs include Gambel oak, Arizona white oak, junipers, mountain mahogany, manzanita and scrub oak.*

Riparian: Riparian vegetation is found along streams, rivers, washes and other water courses, and consists mostly of broad-leaved trees and shrubs. There is also an abundance of grasses, wildflowers and annual plants. Some of the larger trees found in a riparian area form a woodland. These large trees can include cottonwoods, sycamores, walnuts, boxelders, ashes and alders. Willows, mesquite, tamarisk, and other shrubs make up an important understory component in the riparian areas of Central Arizona. Riparian habitats occur at all elevations from the desert to the high mountains.

Edge Habitat: In areas where one type of vegetation merges with another, an edge habitat is created. Because of the greater variety of plant species, these areas are likely to have more kinds of wildlife; some animals prefer edge habitat to any single vegetation type.

In the central Arizona uplands, we are fortunate that fragments of natural habitat have been preserved and are now incorporated into our cities and towns. Many of these cities and towns are also adjacent to national forest, Bureau of Land Management, and Arizona state lands. For these reasons, our region is rich in wildlife species. Wildlife habitats are modified as housing developments, businesses, and roads take over what was once wild and natural land. Often, little forethought or planning has been done to examine how development will affect wildlife.

Urbanization modifies, deteriorates and consumes wildlife habitat. Often native trees, shrubs and other plants are removed. Vegetation communities are altered. Soils are compacted by cars, people and building machines; this disrupts habitat for burrowing animals, and alters the soil conditions, making them unfavorable for native vegetation. Buildings are erected and water courses are altered, destroying riparian vegetation, increasing erosion, and changing the rate of water run off. Air and water pollution increase. If an area becomes highly developed, the concentration of buildings, roads, parking lots and other surfaces changes the absorption and radiation of heat, altering natural temperature patterns.

These changes to the natural landscape alter wildlife habitat in ways that favor some species and work against others. Even though a developed area may have no resemblance to its natural state, it will continue to support those animals with the ability to adapt to the changing habitat. Lawns and gardens provide forage for rabbits, and the accompanying increase in insects provides food for birds and small mammals. Houses offer shelter for birds, and ornamental landscaping creates food and shelter for squirrels, birds and small mammals. As mentioned above, wildlife habitat is a combination of factors that provides suitable life requirements for a given species. Animals that live in urban environments are those that are the most adaptable and the most flexible with their food, water and shelter needs. Some of these are exotic species which have been introduced from other places and have been successful at establishing themselves because of their ability to adapt, and to out-compete native animals. Competition from non-natives and alteration of wildlife habitat greatly decrease species diversity, favor non-native animals, and sometimes consume the habitat of imperiled species.

It is possible to maintain wildlife habitat within our urban areas with careful development, planning, and a sensitivity toward maintaining natural conditions. Protecting wildlife habitat and encouraging native populations of plants and animals conserves our wildlife heritage. It also benefits people by maintaining the natural beauty of an area and enhances the potential for recreational wildlife viewing. People have an innate need to be close to nature. Maintaining urban wildlife habitat helps to fulfill this essential human need. Vital natural habitats within our urban areas reflect an ecologically rich environment which is a healthy and beautiful place for people and animals to live.

Attracting and Encouraging Wildlife

Some residents like to encourage wildlife to come to their homes and yards. However, caution must be taken in the ways that we attract animals to our yards or we will create problems for ourselves, our neighbors and the animals. We must intentionally and purposefully manage how we attract wildlife. Attempts to attract wildlife can produce unexpected results. Feeding birds usually brings squirrels and if feeders are not properly placed and maintained they will also attract skunks, javelina and mice. The unexpected animal visitors are usually the ones that create the problems. By following a few simple guidelines for attracting animals, we can enjoy them without risking the problems. Intentional design, controlled access, and moderation in feeding are keys to the responsible and enjoyable attraction of wildlife.

Even though animals may already live in your yard, you may want to increase their presence or bring them out of hiding to get a better look. A well-designed yard will attract more animal species and may increase their abundance. A landscaping plan with a diversity of vegetation structure will make your property more attractive to a wider spectrum of animals. A good mixture of vegetation includes patches of shrubs, openings, stands of tall trees, mowed areas and uncut native vegetation. A variety of vegetation types is also important. For instance, some animals are attracted to evergreen trees while others need tall grass and herbaceous plants. The drawing on page 14 shows one possible design which provides food, water, cover and a diversity of habitats for attracting urban wildlife.

It is important to create barriers to channel the movement of animals and keep them out of areas where they are unwanted. Garbage cans, compost piles, gardens, crawl spaces, sheds and other areas must be properly managed to avert potential wildlife problems. It is absolutely essential that you control access to certain parts of your property while you are attempting to attract wildlife. Gardens must be fenced; compost piles must be maintained and properly enclosed; garbage cans should be

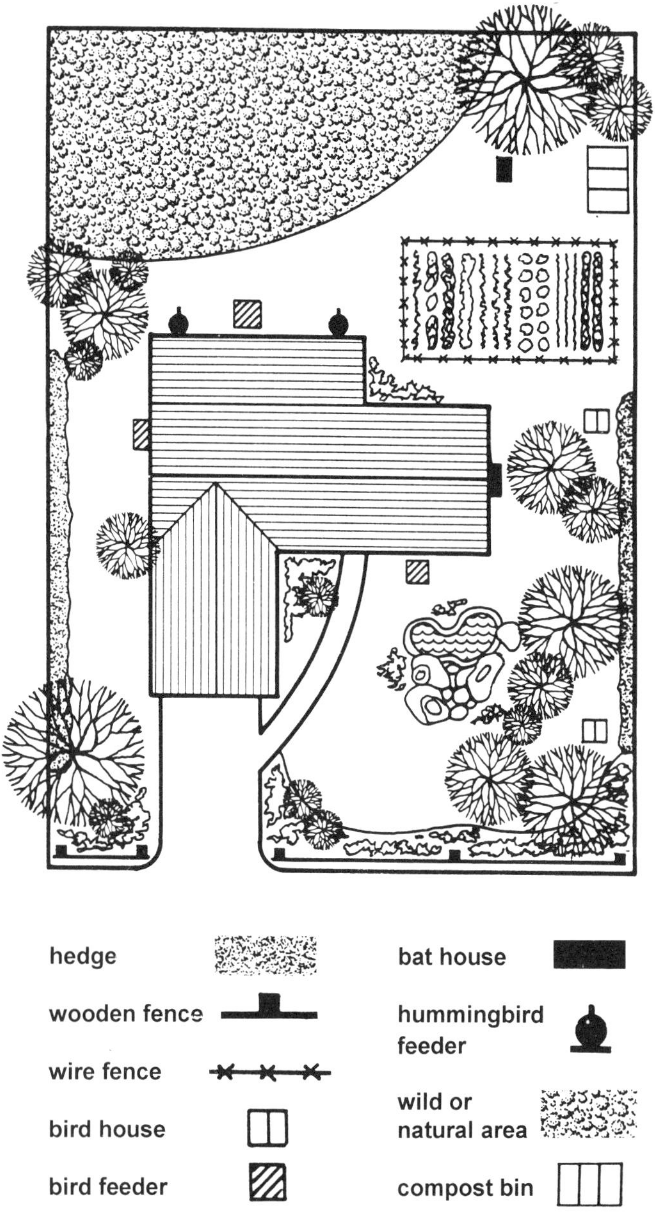

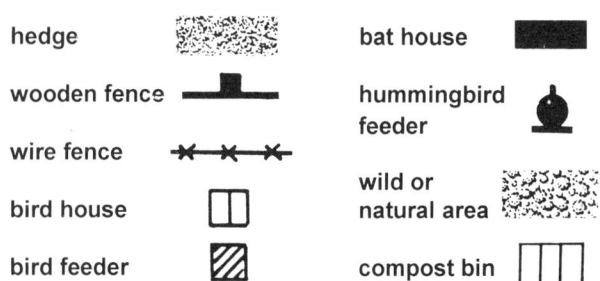

hedge	▒▒▒	bat house	■
wooden fence	—■—	hummingbird feeder	♦
wire fence	×—×—×		
bird house	▯	wild or natural area	▒▒▒
bird feeder	▨	compost bin	▭▭▭

weighted, tied down, or stored in a rack. Otherwise you will find that attracting wildlife works to your detriment. Flower beds must be elevated, fenced, or planted with unpalatable plants. For suggestions on specific trees, shrubs and plants contact your local garden center, county agricultural extension office, or refer to Appendix B for further reading.

The easiest and most effective way to attract wildlife is with a bird feeder. Whether simple or elaborate in construction, bird feeders are a sure bet for attracting wildlife to your yard. To attract a wide variety of birds use several types of feeders. Platform feeders will attract the most species, including ground-feeding birds such as sparrows, doves and jays. Hanging feeders with short perches will give the smaller birds a place to feed when chased away from the platform feeder, and suet baskets will attract the insectivorous birds such as titmice, wrens and woodpeckers. A nectar feeder will bring you many hours of pleasure watching hummingbirds. Cleanliness of feeders is important, since bird food will become moldy or rancid over time. The buildup of bird droppings on feeders is also a problem since this can promote the spread of avian diseases. It is also important to keep the areas beneath your feeders from accumulating spilt food. Spilt birdseed will attract problem animals such as mice, javelina and squirrels. For more information on feeding birds contact your local Audubon Society or refer to Appendix B for further reading.

Some animals should be fed only from native vegetation or from ornamental trees and shrubs. Putting out food to attract mammals will only lead to problems.

Making your yard more attractive to animals is simple if you focus on the factors that determine wildlife habitat. Here are some ideas for enhancing the availability of food, water and cover.

To attract wildlife by increasing food sources:

• Plant trees and shrubs that produce abundant fruit, nuts or seeds (i.e., pyracantha, scrub oak, mountain mahogany, fruit trees).
• Plant wildflowers to attract hummingbirds, insects and insect-eating birds.
• Rake together piles of acorns and other fruit from natural vegetation.
• Set up feeding stations for squirrels; this may keep them from dominating bird feeders.
• Do not throw table scraps in the yard. They will attract unwanted species such as mice, rats, javelina and skunks.

To attract wildlife by increasing water sources:

• Put a bird bath in your yard. Bird baths can be a good source of water for birds and small mammals. If placed on a pedestal, a bird bath must be securely anchored, so that larger animals such as javelina cannot tip it over.
• Build small depressions, or small rock dams in dry washes or drainages.
• Place pools, ponds, or tubs of water at ground level to attract wildlife—but be aware that these can contribute to nuisance problems and should be eliminated if you have unwanted visitors.
• Equip all water sources with an escape route for small animals that may fall into the water. Make a ramp by placing in the water a weighted stick or board that leads to the edge of the pool.

To attract wildlife by increasing shelter and cover:

• Plant a variety of vegetation to offer more diverse cover.

• Provide evergreen trees for year-round hiding places.

• Include deciduous trees which are important feeding places for birds and reptiles and hunting perches for hawks and ravens.

• Plant dense shrubs which create hiding places for snakes, lizards, rabbits and birds.

• Plant vines such as Virginia creeper or wild grape to give cover to small birds such as house finches and sparrows.

• Leave natural areas where groundcover is not cut (i.e., grasses and herbaceous plants).

• Stack rocks in piles of varying sizes to attract lizards, small mammals, snakes and insects.

• Create small piles of brush, away from your house, to serve as shelter and den sites for reptiles, birds, and small mammals. Brush piles are most effective on larger pieces of property where they can be placed at a distance from the house to avoid problems with snakes or mice (brush piles often attract snakes, and should not be used if you do not want snakes or if venomous snakes become a problem).

• Plant hedgerows and windbreaks of large trees on the boundary of your property to create shelter for wintering animals.

• Hang nest boxes in your yard to attract birds and squirrels. See Appendix B for bird books with construction plans.

• Place a bat roost box in your yard. See Appendix B for references on bats.

• Leave dead trees standing when possible. They provide homes for woodpeckers, other cavity-nesting birds and bats. Dead standing trees are important feeding sites for insect-eating animals. Birds of prey also use them for hunting perches.

Managing Urban Wildlife Conflict

Over the past three decades, the central Arizona uplands have changed in many ways. Most of these changes are the result of increasing urban populations. New homes, businesses, roads, shopping centers, and, in many areas, whole new communities now occupy what was once natural wildlife habitat. As the human population has increased, so has the interaction between people and wildlife. Most human/wildlife encounters result in positive, educational and enjoyable experiences. The presence of wildlife in our backyards brightens our day and adds to the pleasure of living close to nature. But when animals take up residence under our homes, dig up our gardens, and damage property, they can become a considerable nuisance. Problems with backyard wildlife range from simple misunderstandings of the animals and their habits to serious property damage and threats to public safety. By paying attention to the wildlife that is around us in cities and towns, by learning a little about its needs and behavior, and by realizing that animals are dependent on the land where we live, we can easily reduce human/wildlife conflict.

Most urban wildlife conflicts can be resolved by being aware of how we unintentionally influence the lives of the animals around us, by changing our behavior, and by making simple modifications that will reduce the elements which attract unwanted animal visitors. As noted earlier, it is important to understand that the animals were here first and that humans have moved into wildlife habitat. Imagine that one morning you woke up to have a huge rock pile suddenly appear in your living room. This must be how it feels to an animal to find a new house in its domain. It is our responsibility to coexist with wildlife and to accept their unobtrusive behavior as a natural part of our surroundings. Keep in mind that the property that we own is important habitat for wildlife.

Animals just do what comes naturally. If residents provide structures that mimic natural shelter, animals will use them. For example, an open crawl space under a home may be an excellent imitation of a cave and will serve as a convenient shelter for a family of striped skunks. When a conflict occurs, it is important to understand that animals are just following their natural inclinations about making a living.

Another concept to remember is that all animals must have food, water and shelter to live, grow and reproduce. Residents unintentionally attract animals by providing convenient sources of food, water and shelter which, in turn, leads to conflict. Removing these attractants, or restricting wildlife access to them, will make your home a less desirable place for wildlife. The majority of problems encountered by homeowners can be resolved simply by understanding how they are unintentionally providing animals an easy living. Trash cans need to be closed and secured, compost needs to be contained in an animal-proof enclosure and pet food and birdseed need to be carefully managed. Excess water must be monitored in open containers, leaking garden hoses, and runoff from drip irrigation. Crawl spaces, outbuildings, attics and house eaves need to be closed off, or otherwise modified, to keep animals out. Gardens must be fenced, and flowers and ornamental shrubs need to be carefully chosen to reduce their appeal as food. In short, if you have a nuisance problem, you need to remove the availability of food, water and shelter.

Modifying your property is one self-help method for

creating a less desirable habitat for problem species. Habitat is easily modified, by fencing to limit access to specific parts of your property, mowing to reduce cover, removing rock piles, brush piles, and weed patches and by elevating firewood piles to eliminate hiding places and possible dens. Other ways to deter wildlife from visiting your home include using repellents and some simple techniques for making your property an unpleasant place for wildlife. Some nontoxic items commonly found in homes, such as ammonia and cayenne pepper, can be used effectively as wildlife repellents. There are also several chemical repellents for small mammals and birds available at garden centers and building supply stores. Simply making it an unpleasant experience for animal visitors will often deter them from returning. Placing statues of predators, banging pots and pans, spraying water, or using wind-driven movement devices such as pinwheels, suspended pie tins, or tinfoil balls, are effective short-term deterrents in some situations.

If the removal of attractants, modification of habitat, and use of repellents have failed, the next course of action is the live trapping and relocation of problem wildlife. Live

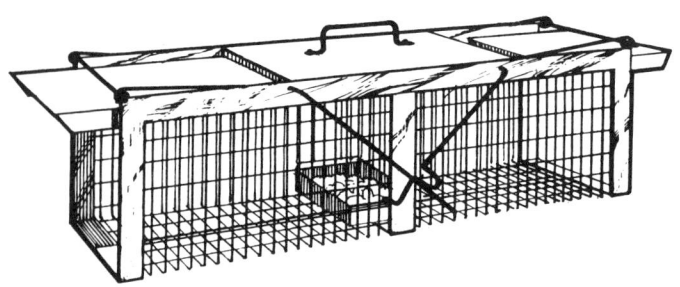

traps capture small animals without harming them. These traps are available in a variety of sizes designed for mice and small rodents up to medium-size dogs. You can find these traps at most animal-feed supply outlets in central Arizona, and, under certain circumstances, you can borrow them from city or county animal-control departments. **Before attempting to live-trap an animal, you must contact the Arizona Game and Fish Department for specific methods, precautions, and locations for release.**

Professional help will be needed to manage wildlife problems that involve sick, poisonous, orphaned, or dangerous animals. You may seek professional assistance from the Arizona Game and Fish Department, city or county wildlife-control departments, professional pest-control companies, the U.S. Forest Service, or the county agricultural extension office. The addresses and telephone numbers for these and other urban-wildlife organizations are in Appendix A. The Arizona Game and Fish Department maintains a list of licensed wildlife-service operators who will, for a fee, remove problem animals from your property. Contact the Arizona Game and Fish Department for the names and phone numbers of the licensed wildlife service operators in your area.

Do not endanger yourself or your family by confronting or cornering a problem animal. If an animal bite occurs, contact your local city or county animal-control department immediately to assess the risk of rabies.

Once you have an animal damaging your property or living in an undesirable place, it may be difficult to resolve the problem. Specific methods for reducing urban-wildlife conflicts can be found under the section for each species. This book advocates the use of nonlethal methods that are easily employed by the homeowner for resolving urban-wildlife conflicts. Being a responsible co-inhabitant means respecting the value of wildlife, conserving wildlife populations and changing your behaviors that are contributing to the problem. Very few urban-wildlife problems require killing animals.

In rare cases, lethal methods such as firearms, traps or poisons may be the only effective solution. The killing of wildlife is strictly regulated by the Arizona Game and Fish Department. Shooting an animal with a firearm in an urban setting is a serious risk to other residents and is usually illegal. It is unlawful to shoot a firearm at wildlife within a quarter-mile of a dwelling without the owner's or occupant's permission. Any other discharge of a firearm may be classified as endangerment. The killing of big-game species for wildlife-problem control is illegal. All nongame birds, except house sparrows, starlings, and feral pigeons, are protected by state and federal laws. Many reptile and amphibian species are protected because of their special status as imperiled species. The taking of other unprotected reptiles and amphibians requires an Arizona hunting license and is subject to strict regulation by the Arizona Game and Fish Department.

If you have an animal-nuisance problem that may require the destruction of any wildlife, your first course of action must be to contact the Arizona Game and Fish Department for the laws governing that species. The use of poisons to control wildlife is not a preferred alternative because of the risk of accidental poisoning of people, pets and other wildlife. When poisons are the only alternative, application should be done only by a professional pest control company. **Killing an animal to solve a nuisance wildlife problem should be reserved for extreme cases where nonlethal methods have been tried and have failed.**

To be responsible co-inhabitants with urban wildlife means that we must work together to keep the best interests of our animal neighbors in mind. Conservation of our wildlife heritage requires that we examine our actions and the effects that they have on the health and well-being of our wildlife populations. One of the greatest threats to small mammals, birds and reptiles is their predation and harassment by domestic cats. Although cats can be difficult to manage, they must be discouraged from killing wildlife. Cat owners may find some success by placing a collar with a bell on the cat. The bell alerts animals to the cat's presence and foils its hunting attempts. Many cats are intolerant of wearing collars and they will need to be replaced frequently. The only certain method for preventing cats from killing wildlife is to keep them well fed and indoors.

Another serious problem facing urban-wildlife species is their dependence on unnatural food sources. Food found around urban areas disrupts the natural distribution of wildlife and causes overpopulation. Concentration of wildlife around unnatural food sources creates a higher potential for disease transmission and causes stressful living conditions by increasing competition and territorial disputes. Garbage, birdseed, leftovers and other unnatural foods do not match the nutritional needs of wild animals and can lead to malnutrition or illness. It may not be a problem for you to attract wildlife by dumping out leftovers or leaving the compost uncovered, but what about your neighbors? The javelina and skunks that you attract will roam your neighbor's property looking for a handout or digging up flower beds. Small acts such as keeping garbage cans tightly covered and carefully managing birdseed will go a long way toward conserving our wildlife for the future and reducing human/wildlife conflict. It is up to all of us to be responsible members of both our human and natural communities.

Backyard
MAMMALS

BACKYARD MAMMALS

Bats
Vespertilionidae and Molossidae families

Characteristics:
Small winged mammals; ears medium to large; wing formed by membrane of skin.

There are at least a dozen species of bats that live in the central Arizona uplands. Most are summer residents and migrate to warmer climates for the winter. They can be found in all the vegetation types of the central Arizona uplands. A few of the more common species include the

tiny western pipistrelle (*Pipistrellus hesperus*) weighing only five or six grams; the big brown bat (*Eptesicus fuscus*) with its reddish fur and fearsome teeth; the gentle pallid bat (*Antrozous pallidus*) that has large wings and big ears; and

the Mexican free-tailed bat (*Tadarida brasiliensis*) which roosts in colonies of hundreds, thousands or even millions, of individuals.

Bats are among the most misunderstood creatures in the world. Perhaps their strange appearance or their nocturnal lifestyle accounts for the misunderstanding, but it is more likely that people fear bats because of their negative portrayal in myth, movies and folklore. Bats are the victims of wildly embellished stories of bloodsucking and disease. These stories are grossly exaggerated or the products of ignorance. The truth is that only three of the nearly 100 species of bats worldwide take blood as a source of nourishment. Bats that take blood primarily use birds and livestock as host species, and live only in South and Central America. Other misconceptions about bats, such as that they aggressively attack people or build nests in women's hair, are simply not true.

Like all mammals, bats are susceptible to rabies, but the notion that all bats are rabid is unfounded. On the contrary, only one-half of one percent of bats contract the disease. This occurrence is no greater than found in other animals such as skunks and foxes. Rabid bats quickly become very sick, and they rarely come into contact with other animals before dying. They are not the cause of rabies outbreaks as once thought. People need to be cautious when interacting with any wild animal. Handling or getting too close to an animal can result in a bite. **Any bat that you can catch is likely to be sick.** If you come across a sick or dead bat, keep your distance and seek the advice of your local wildlife manager before taking any action.

Like people, bats are mammals. They produce milk and suckle young; have fur (hair); give birth to live babies and maintain a constant body temperature. They also have some truly astounding adaptations that make them very special creatures. Bats are the only mammals with wings and the ability of true flight. The skeletal structure of a bat's wing is equivalent to the bones of your arms and hands. A thin membrane of skin stretches between the fingers, arm bones and body to form the wing. Bats are swift and accurate flyers and many species catch insects in flight.

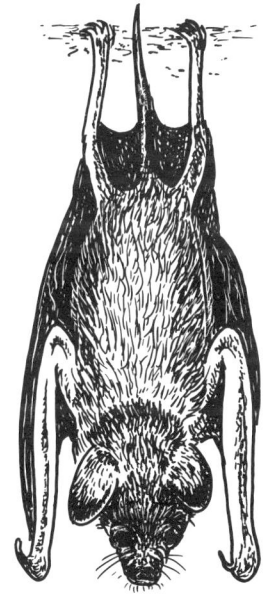

Perhaps the most astounding adaptation of bats is their ability to use high-frequency sounds to navigate, avoid obstacles and capture prey. Called echolocation, this technique is similar to the sonar used by ships to avoid underwater hazards. Bats produce high-frequency sounds (above the audible range of humans) from their vocal cords. When the sound strikes an object it is echoed back to the bat's sensitive ears. From these reflected sounds bats can determine the size, shape, texture, movement, speed and distance of an object. Just as you and I form images from what we see, bats form ultrasonic images of their surroundings with echolocation. Incidentally, bats are not blind—most species can see quite well.

Bats are nocturnal and spend their days resting in the shelter of caves and mine shafts, under the bark of trees, in rock crevices, in attics, under the eaves of houses and among the foliage of larger broad-leaved trees. All of the bats in our range eat insects and other small invertebrates. They take flight in the early evening in search of scorpions, spiders, moths and other flying insects. Bats catch great quantities of flying insects by grabbing them with their feet or mouths and by scooping them up with their wings. Bats play an important role in controlling insect populations and eat many pest species, including mosquitoes. Biologists have estimated that a single Mexican free-tailed bat can consume up to 600 mosquitoes in an hour!

Bats roost alone, in small groups, or in large colonies. Roosts serve as resting places during the day, as shelter during hibernation, and as maternity colonies where young are born and cared for. Some species prefer human structures to natural roosts or relocate to these structures when their natural roosts are disturbed or destroyed. Attics, loose siding, shutters, chimneys, vents and the eaves of houses serve as good roost sites for bats. When bats locate their roost sites in attics, walls or chimneys, their squeaking, scratching and crawling can be a nuisance. The odor from fecal droppings and urine can become objectionable as well.

Ridding yourself of unwanted bats is a matter of timing. Exclusion of bats from a structure should be done in the fall after the young can fly from the roost. Holes should be closed off in the evening after the bats have left. Cover all entrances except the most prominent one. For this entrance, construct a one-way door from which the bats may leave, but not reenter.

On occasion a bat will appear inside someone's home. Usually it enters through an open window or door, or through a chimney or loose-fitting screen door. Removing a bat from your home can be quite nerve-racking, but don't panic. The bat's swoops and dives are its efforts to escape and not an attempt to attack you. Open the doors and windows and try chasing it out. If this does not work, wait for it to become tired; it will eventually come to rest. Now you can capture the 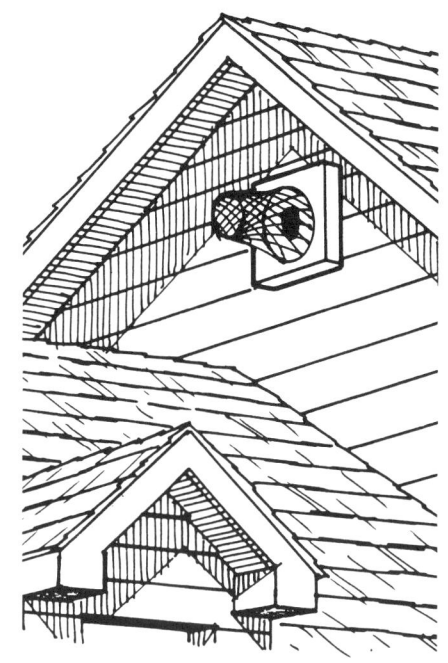 bat by carefully placing a jar or coffee can over it. Then slide a piece of cardboard over the opening of the container and carry it out of the house. Do not, under any circumstances, handle a bat without wearing leather work gloves.

The greatest threats to bats are the disturbance of maternity colonies and hibernation roosts and the loss of roost sites for cave-dwelling bats. Most of the species of bats that are in trouble are dependent on caves and mine shafts for a large portion of their lives. Careless cave exploration and intentional persecution have put several bat species on the verge of extinction. In the spring and early summer females of some species of bats congregate in large colonies where they give birth and nurse their young. What may appear to be a harmless disturbance by a cave explorer will, in fact, be a devastating blow to the colony. Mother bats will take flight when startled and, as a result, drop the young who cannot fly. The young die from the blow of the fall or from starvation. Hibernating bats are equally vulnerable to disturbance. If bats are aroused during hibernation, they burn up large amounts of stored fat attempting to escape. In the winter there are no insects for a bat to eat in order to resupply critical energy reserves. Without stored energy the bats quickly starve or freeze to death.

Bats are a valuable part of your backyard ecology. You can attract them by installing a light that concentrates insects, or by installing a bat roost box available from Bat Conservation International (See Appendix A). Once the veil of fear and ignorance is lifted, we can appreciate bats for the remarkable and likeable creatures that they are.

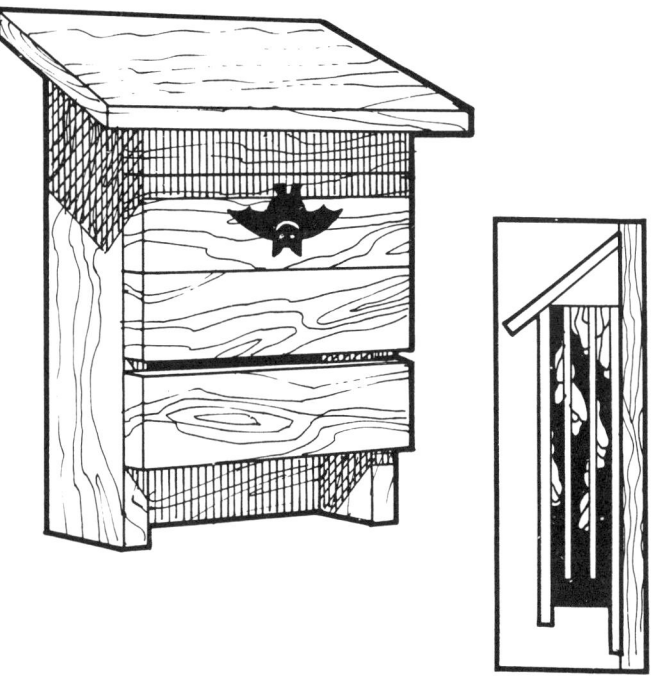

Cottontail
Sylvilagus spp.

Characteristics:
A medium-sized rabbit; long ears; long hind feet; whitish underparts; underside of tail white; grayish to brownish above.

Cottontail rabbits are abundant in the chaparral and pinyon/juniper woodlands throughout the central Arizona uplands. They are also present, but less common, in the pine forests. Look for cottontails in areas that have tall grass and shrubs. Here they can hide from predators and find a meal. Cottontails are most active at dawn and dusk.

As strict vegetarians, cottontails eat a variety of plant material including leaves, stems, flowers, roots, buds and

bark. In the spring and summer a cottontail's diet consists primarily of tender new plant growth. As summer yields to fall and winter, they browse the woody stems of trees and shrubs.

Cottontails have acute senses of hearing and sight. Their large ears act as sound collectors and can be rotated independently of the head. This allows the rabbit to pick up the slightest noise from any direction. A cottontail's look of innocence comes from its large bulging eyes, which provide a panoramic view of nearly 360 degrees. These sensory adaptations keep cottontails alert and ready to employ their best defense mechanism—fast, unpredictable, zigzagging leaps, hops and bounds that take them to the cover of dense brush or into a burrow. The burrows, dug by badgers, skunks and other animals, are also used for nesting.

Hawks, owls, bobcats and coyotes are the greatest threats to adult cottontails, and snakes have been known to prey on cottontail young. Although there are many dangers in a rabbit's life, cottontails are very prolific. Cottontails have several litters of four to six young per year, and females born early in the spring can breed that same year.

Like all rabbits, cottontail young are born hairless and blind. This is one of the traits that separates rabbits from hares such as jackrabbits. Mothers nurse the young only twice a day, but the babies grow fast. In ten to twenty days, the baby cottontails are ready to leave the nest, and in about five weeks they are able to care for themselves.

Cottontails delight in the opportunity to dine on unprotected vegetable gardens, flower beds and sapling trees. If you grow vegetables you are probably well aware of the damage that a persistent cottontail can cause. An unfenced garden is an open invitation for wildlife to browse on what is available, just as they would do in their natural habitat. Fencing is generally effective to keep cottontails out. Fencing must be three feet high and must be buried six to twelve inches below ground to prevent the rabbits from digging under it. Wooden fences will need a sheet-metal barrier attached along the bottom to prevent the rabbits from gnawing gaps in the fence. Sapling trees can be protected by constructing a cylinder of hardware cloth around them. You can also deter cottontails by keeping your yard and adjacent areas mowed and cleared of vegetation around the base of shrubs. Rabbits avoid areas that lack enough cover for them to hide from predators. Ammonia-soaked rags placed near nesting areas and dens may be effective in repelling cottontails. Commercial rabbit repellents are also available at garden shops. These chemical repellents need to be applied often and are for flowers and other inedible plants only.

Rock Squirrel
Spermophilus variegatus

Characteristics:
A large ground squirrel; dappled fur is red to brown at the head and shoulder, gray at the back, gray to buff at the rump and white to tan below.

Rock squirrels are uncommonly large for ground squirrels. They are nearly the size of tree squirrels, but live on the ground and do not often climb or nest in trees. They

live in every elevation from the low desert to the high pine forest and are abundant throughout our range. As their name suggests, rock squirrels live on and around rocks, in canyons, outcrops and boulder fields. They are most active in the early morning and late afternoon. You can easily identify them by their high-pitched, whistle-like, calls.

Rock squirrels eat nuts, seeds, buds, fruit, and carrion. After collecting food, they store a large portion of it in the den. Rock squirrels dig their dens among the rocks, making it difficult for predators to dig them out. Bobcats, coyotes, red-tailed hawks and golden eagles are the greatest threats to rock squirrels. Predators have a difficult time catching the squirrels because they are always alert, and at the slightest suspicion of danger, they quickly escape to the safety of the rocks. Rock squirrels spend the coldest part of the winter dormant in their dens. Whether they actually hibernate or not is uncertain, but it is known that on warm winter days they sometimes emerge to feed.

Despite their ground-dwelling habits, rock squirrels are good climbers. On occasion they will climb a juniper tree to pick its berries. They will also climb onto a bird feeder that is not suspended. In addition, rock squirrels are adept at leaping onto a feeder that is hanging close to a tree trunk or porch railing. A separate feeding station for the squirrels will keep them at bay for a while, but they will eventually return to the bird feeder. There are many devices commercially available to keep squirrels out of bird feeders. Some of them are better than others, but none of them is foolproof. Contact your local Audubon Society, or refer to one of the many field guides to attracting birds for more information on which devices are the most effective. A cone-shaped sheet metal

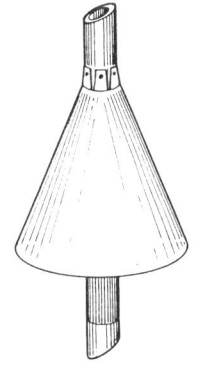

baffle, suspended on a wire, string, or pole supporting a hanging feeder, will prevent squirrels from climbing down the wire to the feeder.

For feeders and bird houses supported by a post, try fastening a two-foot length of six-inch diameter aluminum vent pipe to the bottom of the feeder platform. The pipe, which encircles the post, is too slippery on the outside for squirrels to climb and the inside dead ends at the feeder platform. *(See drawing to the right.)*

Another device (*illustrated below*) to discourage squirrels can be made by placing a loosely-fitting disk made of metal or wood on the post, supported with a flange. When a squirrel attempts to climb around the disk, the metal or wooden piece tips easily and startles the animal.

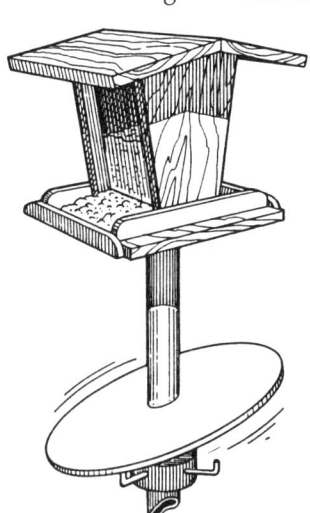

Rock squirrels are an excellent example of how it is difficult to attract one type of animal without attracting others. Where there is bird seed there will be squirrels. Try to enjoy them as a natural part of the habitat in which you live.

BACKYARD MAMMALS

Abert's Squirrel
Sciurus aberti

Characteristics:
A large tree squirrel; gray with reddish coloring on back; bushy tail is grizzled gray and white; ears have tassels.

The Abert's squirrel is also called the "tassel-eared squirrel" because of the tufts of fur that grow upon its ears in the winter. Abert's squirrels are common residents of the

pine forests of the central Arizona uplands. They are endemic to the pine-covered areas on and below the Mogollon rim. Since the 1940s these squirrels have been introduced to several other locales around the state including the Bradshaw Mountains and Mingus Mountain. Abert's squirrels now live in all the ponderosa pine forests in this region.

The life of an Abert's squirrel is centered around the ponderosa pine tree. They live and nest among the branches and feed on the trees' buds, flowers, bark and seeds. Other food items of the Abert's squirrel, such as insects, mistletoe berries, and truffles, live in or grow under the ponderosa pine. The best evidence that Abert's squirrels are nearby is the refuse that they drop from trees when feeding. In the summer months, after eating the tender seeds and pine cone bracts, the squirrels drop the cores of the cones to the ground. In the winter, Abert's squirrels supplement their diet with the soft innerbark from the ends of pine branches. While harvesting the bark, the squirrels clip the ends of the branches and litter the ground below with the brush-like pine needle clusters. Abert's squirrels build ball-shaped nests in the branches of larger ponderosa pines. In the nest they raise young, escape inclement weather, and sleep.

The only common predators of Abert's squirrels are Northern goshawks and human hunters. When threatened, an Abert's squirrel will hide by flattening itself to a limb. The squirrel's fur blends with the tree bark, making it difficult to see. Abert's squirrels are active year-round and can be found basking in the sun on winter mornings. In the summer, they arch their tails over their backs. The white color of the tail reflects the sun rays and helps keep the squirrel cool.

Female Abert's squirrels are capable of mating for only eighteen hours each year. In April or May, when the females are in heat, a mating chase begins. A group of male squirrels follows the female as she races about the forest leaping from tree to tree. After hours of pursuit, she is eventually forced to the apex of a tree where she mates with several males. After a forty-day gestation period, two to four young are born. They develop rapidly and become independent about twenty days after birth.

Pocket Gopher
Thomomys bottae

Characteristics:
A medium-sized rodent; thick body; naked tail; long claws; small ears and small eyes; fur reddish-brown to dark black.

Pocket gophers can be found throughout our region and in all of our vegetation types. They live in areas with soils suitable for digging tunnels. Although gophers are

relatively common, few people have ever seen a pocket gopher because they spend most of their lives underground. What is commonly seen are the mounds of dirt that gophers push to the surface when digging their burrows.

Pocket gophers dig their burrows parallel to the ground surface. The burrows consist of a permanent main tunnel with several less-permanent side branches. The main tunnel is the heart of a gopher's territory. It provides access to the side tunnels where the gopher digs for food, nests, stockpiles food, and deposits the tailings of its excavations. The side tunnels also lead to entrances and exits.

Pocket gophers are well adapted to living in their underground world. They have sharp, elongated claws and strong front legs for tunneling. Their powerful front teeth easily cut roots and dig through the dirt. A gopher's incisors grow nine to fourteen inches per year. Continual digging and gnawing wear the teeth down, maintaining them at a manageable length. A gopher's body is cylindrical which allows it to move easily through the tunnels. In the underground world of a gopher the sense of touch is the most important. As a result, pocket gophers have small, underdeveloped eyes, and small, rounded ears that tuck neatly back against the head.

Many plants that live in arid environments, such as those of the central Arizona uplands, store moisture in roots and tubers. Pocket gophers eat these moist underground parts of plants. The roots and tubers supply gophers with nourishment and most of their water needs. Gophers also eat herbs, grasses, bulbs and other plant material.

Pocket gophers live alone in their burrows. Males enter the burrows of females during brief periods of mating in the early spring. Females produce a single litter of one to seven young per year. When the young leave the nest they travel aboveground and dig a new burrow in an area adjacent to the mother's.

Backyard gophers can be a difficult problem to contend with. Once they are established, they are difficult to get rid of. Most nonlethal methods of removing gophers from vegetable gardens are not effective. You can try collapsing gopher burrows or flooding them with water as a short term deterrent. Unfortunately, if you want to effectively remove gophers from your garden you will need to use traps, poisons or chemical fumigants. The latter two methods require the help of a licensed pest-control specialist. The traps are available at most garden centers. They are easy to set and are usually effective at killing the gophers. After the gophers have been removed, you can prevent them from returning by constructing a barrier of half-inch hardware cloth. Bury the wire mesh, standing vertically, three feet deep (or to bedrock) and encircling the perimeter of your garden.

To keep gophers from getting into your lawn and flower bulbs, try burying hardware cloth horizontally and twelve inches below the surface. Extend the mesh twelve inches beyond the edge of the planting area. In this case the depth of the mesh is important. If it is not buried deeply enough, the roots will extend far below the mesh where the gophers can reach them. If the mesh is buried too deeply, the gophers will be able to burrow above it. When constructing raised-bed gardens, nail wire mesh across the bottom of the forms that hold the soil in place. This barrier will deny access by gophers, but still allow for the movement of water and soil nutrients.

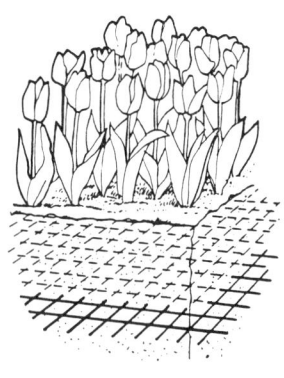

Beaver
Castor canadensis

Characteristics:
A very large rodent; broad paddle-like tail; webbed hind feet; dense fur; large, thick incisors.

Historically, beavers were common along most of the rivers in the state. Their populations were greatly reduced by heavy trapping during the 1800s, the diversion of wa-

ter, human encroachment on their habitat, and the decline of quality streamside habitat. Today beavers are uncommon residents of northern and central Arizona. In our area, beavers are found only along the Verde River and its larger tributaries.

Beavers are the largest rodents in North America and can weigh as much as sixty pounds. They are specifically adapted for swimming and have valved ears, webbed feet, and a paddle-like tail. A beaver's fur is long and thick to insulate against the cold of its aquatic life. They are industrious creatures and have strong jaws and sharp teeth for gnawing and cutting down trees. Beavers eat the tender saplings of cottonwood and aspen trees, the inner bark of larger trees, the bark, foliage, and tender wood of willows, and the underground parts of tuberous plants.

Beavers dam smaller streams to insure a year-round supply of water for transporting food and materials. They construct the dams from logs, sticks, rocks and other debris. The beavers use their strong, sharp incisors to cut down trees. They then float, push and roll the wood into a mound large enough to form a dam. Sometimes beavers also build a stick-lodge den as part, or independent of the dam structure. Along larger rivers, they dig burrows into the bank. In either case, beavers enter the dens from below the water to an internal cavity that is above the high-water line.

Beavers cut many trees for the construction of dams and lodges and to reach the tender bark, buds and foliage for food. The cutting of trees may seem destructive, but the enterprising activities of the beaver play an important role in streamside ecology. Pools formed by the dam create a wetland habitat for many animals and plants including fish, waterfowl, willows and cattails. They also slow the fast-moving water and trap sediment, which in turn reduces erosion. Eventually, the entire pond will silt in, and the beavers will abandon the area. As the old pond dries out, grasses take over and a meadow forms. This new habitat becomes home for another set of animals such as deer, turkeys and pocket gophers. In forested areas, the openings made by beavers create forest-edge habitat that is important for songbirds and squirrels. The cutting of aspen trees actually revitalizes the stand by stimulating new growth.

Beavers love the sweet sap of fruit trees and other ornamental trees. If you live along the Verde River where the beavers are active, you will need to protect your landscaping. Plant your trees and shrubs away from the stream or river. Wrapping tree trunks with a stiff wire mesh buried at least six inches into the ground, and three feet above the ground, will deter the beavers. Be sure that the mesh is not too tight, or the beavers may still be able to gnaw at the bark with their long incisors.

BACKYARD MAMMALS

Woodrat
Neotoma spp.

Characteristics:
A medium-sized rat; long tail is lighter on the underside; large eyes; naked ears; and white underparts and feet.

Commonly called "packrats," woodrats live in the pinyon/juniper and chaparral of the central Arizona uplands. Unlike the Norway, or sewer rat, woodrats are native to North America. Woodrats are easily distinguished from their European cousins by their light brown fur, hairy tails and large ears.

Woodrats eat cactus, mesquite beans, juniper berries, pinyon nuts, foliage, and tender branches of shrubs. The succulent pads of prickly pear and other cacti provide up to ninety percent of a woodrat's water needs. Woodrats are active at dusk and dawn, and remain so year-round. Their predators include coyotes, foxes, ringtails, skunks, owls, and snakes.

Woodrats live in large dens constructed from sticks, cactus, leaves, cow dung, litter, and other materials. Dens are assembled around the base of a tree or shrub or in a rock crevice, cave or building. Great mounds up to three feet high and eight feet in diameter can accumulate from the rats' incessant construction. Inside the den woodrats store food in an area called a midden, and build a nest lined with finely shredded grasses. American Indians once robbed woodrat food stores for their large accumulations of pinyon nuts. Entrances to the den are often fortified with cactus spines. Cholla and prickly-pear cacti that are used in the den's structure are also eaten as a convenient food source. Other rodents, lizards and snakes find shelter in the spacious debris pile of woodrat dens.

When transporting an object to the den, a woodrat might happen upon something more appealing. In this case, it will drop the first object and continue with the new one. This behavior has led to the name "trade rat" as another of the woodrat's titles. Woodrats like shiny objects, and if a woodrat collects its materials indoors, it will sometimes take valuable objects. Watches, silverware, coins, and jewelry have all been found in woodrat dens. In Arizona's arid climate, abandoned woodrat dens decay very slowly. Old dens that were preserved in caves and under rock ledges have revealed clues to what local vegetation was like thousands of years ago at the time the dens were constructed.

Woodrats are a problem when they build their nests in an attic, under a mobile home, in a shed, in a barn or under the hood of a vehicle. You can try hanging lights, playing loud music, or placing ammonia-soaked rags around the nest. If this is not effective in repelling the rats from the area, you may need to trap them. Live traps are usually effective for woodrats. These nonlethal traps can be purchased at animal feed and hardware stores. In addition, several of the city and county animal-control offices lend traps to residents. Promptly disassembling and removing a den will keep the rats from coming back. For dens built inside a structure, you will need to close off the entrance holes that the woodrats are using. In most cases a combination of repellents, traps, and regular disturbance will be effective in evicting your unwanted guests. If woodrats are eating your garden or other plants, try surrounding the plants with a two-foot-tall sheet-metal barrier. Sprinkling blood meal on the ground will also help keep the rats away, and at the same time it will fertilize your soil.

BACKYARD MAMMALS

Coyote
Canis latrans

Characteristics:
A medium-sized doglike mammal; grizzled gray to buff above; whitish below; bushy tail has black tip.

Coyotes are common throughout the western United States, and live in all of the vegetation types of the central Arizona uplands. They are one of the few animals that have actually profited from human expansion. Coyotes have

increased their range and colonized new habitats. Their populations are larger now than before European settlement.

The coyote's success is largely due to its adaptable nature. When its diet of rodents, rabbits, birds, snakes or lizards is not available, a coyote will eat carrion, beetles, grasshoppers, garbage, cactus fruit or other plant material. Packs of coyotes prey on young or weak deer, elk and pronghorn. In urban and rural areas, they find chickens, geese, domestic cats and small dogs to be easy prey. They may sometimes attack young sheep and cattle. Coyotes' adaptability is not limited to their omnivorous diet. They occupy a wide range of habitats and are as much at home in the pine forest as they are in the desert scrub.

Some people regard coyotes as notorious predators because they occasionally kill livestock and young game animals. As a result, hundreds of thousands of coyotes have been killed in an attempt to eradicate them. Coyotes have been shot from the ground, shot from planes and helicopters, trapped and poisoned. Most of these attempts at reducing coyote populations have not worked. Other coyotes quickly replaced the ones that were killed. There is great uncertainty about how often coyotes actually prey on sheep and cattle. When the contents of hundreds of coyote stomachs were examined, only a small percentage contained the flesh of sheep or cattle. In many cases where the remains of livestock were found in the stomachs of coyotes, it was impossible to tell whether the meat was consumed from a freshly killed animal or from carrion.

Other people find the coyote to be an inspiring symbol of the starry nights and open spaces of the American Southwest. Coyotes embody such admirable human qualities as freedom and resiliency. In the legends of some American Indian cultures, the coyote is the trickster. This sometimes wise and sometimes foolish character teaches us how to laugh at our mistakes, and how to persevere in the face of adversity.

Coyote pairs have a strong bond, and once established, it may last for several years. Mating occurs in early spring. Five or six young are born and nurtured in a den dug into the ground or nestled among rocks. The mother coyote nurses the young pups and as they mature both parents feed them by disgorging partially digested food. In eight to 10 weeks the pups are weaned and the family begins to move about their territory. As the youngsters grow, the family hunts together as a pack. The juvenile coyotes grow stronger, wiser and more self-sufficient, and in six to nine months they disperse to establish their own territories.

In rural areas and on the edges of cities and towns, coyotes find unsecured garbage cans and house cats to offer easy meals. In most parts of the central Arizona uplands, it is smart to protect your cats by keeping them indoors at night. Secure your garbage-can lids with a weight, or strap the cans down. It is also wise to keep pet food and other potential attractants out of the reach of coyotes.

The coyote's song starts with a few sharp barks and ends in a long ascending howl. Yips, barks and howls increase as distant replies form a coyote chorus. The coyote's serenade evokes the mystery of the night. It reminds us of their undaunted will to survive and that the coyote is here to stay.

Gray Fox
Urocyon cinereoargenteus

Characteristics:
A doglike animal smaller than a coyote; grizzled gray above; reddish on neck, underside and back of ears; bushy tail is black on ridge and tip.

The gray fox is at home in the grasslands, chaparral and pinyon/juniper woodlands. They prefer the rough, broken country of open woodlands and rocky areas. Gray foxes are also present, but less common, in the pine forest. They

live throughout most of North America and are fairly common in the central Arizona uplands.

As gray foxes hunt and forage, they routinely travel the same paths nightly. In urban areas, they use the creek beds as travel corridors. Foxes are primarily nocturnal, but are often moving about at dusk and dawn. They eat rodents, cottontails, grasshoppers, birds, lizards, snakes, cactus fruit and the berries of manzanitas and junipers.

Gray foxes are agile, smart and patient. They hunt more like cats than like their canine relatives. Foxes will patiently stalk a cottontail and wait for the right moment to pounce. They pin their prey to the ground with their front paws and then bite to kill it. Also like cats, foxes can climb trees to escape danger or to just rest.

Where the soil allows, gray foxes dig dens into the ground. They also den in mine shafts, crevices, cavities among boulders, and sometimes in hollow trees. Gray foxes breed in the spring and have one to seven young in each litter. The pups spend the first two to three months in the den. After that, they accompany the mother on hunting trips learning to capture prey. A gray fox family occupies a distinct home range of about two square miles. To warn invaders of their territorial boundaries, foxes create "scent posts" by defecating on logs and rocks.

The predators of foxes include golden eagles, coyotes, bobcats and humans. Since the 1800s, trappers have pursued gray foxes for their attractive pelts. Even today, they remain a popular trap animal. If gray foxes can escape their predators, they may live to be fifteen years old.

BACKYARD MAMMALS

Raccoon
Procyon lotor

Characteristics:
A medium-sized gray mammal with long legs, a broad head, a ringed tail and a black mask.

Raccoons live throughout North America. They are not dependent on any particular vegetation type, but they tend to avoid the high mountains and dry deserts. Raccoons rarely stray far from permanent water. In the central Arizona uplands they are most commonly found along riparian waterways and near the edges of towns and cities.

Raccoons are curious, intelligent and adaptable creatures. They are sometimes referred to as "masked bandits" because of the black band across their eyes and their propensity for mischievous behavior. They can use their paws almost like human hands. This allows them to open garbage cans, screen doors, backpacks, coolers and almost anything else that might harbor a convenient meal.

A raccoon's front paws are specially adapted for grasping. Each one has five fingers which is an uncommon trait among carnivores. The skin on the palm of a raccoon's paw is soft and sensitive, giving it an acute sense of touch. Raccoons hunt by feeling for prey on the bottom of streams and lakes. Once the prey is captured, the raccoon manipulates it in its hands under the surface of the water. This gives the appearance that the raccoon is washing its food before eating it. This action, however, is more likely to be a tactile examination of the item and the water probably enhances the raccoon's sense of touch.

Raccoons are opportunistic omnivores. In other words, they will eat just about anything that is edible, although, when food is abundant, they are selective feeders and prefer crawfish, frogs, fish and beetle grubs. When food is less abundant they will adapt by eating nuts, berries, foliage, insects, birdseed, garbage or carrion. Raccoons put on fat during the summer and fall in preparation for winter. They can easily double their body weight during this time, but the fat is all lost during the lean times of winter.

In colder climates, raccoons spend the winter in a dormant state akin to hibernation. Stored fat is burned to keep the animal warm, but unlike true hibernation, the raccoon's body temperature never drops below normal. The raccoons of the central Arizona uplands remain active year-round because of our mild climate.

Raccoons nest in crevices and cavities in cliffs, between boulders and in hollow trees. Mating occurs year-round and three to five cubs are born to each litter. About two weeks after the cubs are born their eyes and ears open, and their facial mask and tail rings become evident. The young raccoons spend the summer and fall taking lessons from their mother on hunting, climbing, and avoiding predators. Just before winter they set out on their own.

The raccoons' eccentric behavior and attractive appearance make them among the most popular of backyard visitors. If you live near the Verde River or one of its tributaries, you have a good chance of seeing raccoons in their natural habitat as well as in town. They will seek out food, water and shelter in human settlements and will easily become accustomed to the lights and noise of an urban area. Be careful if you attempt to attract raccoons to your yard. Their casual visits can become a nuisance, to you and your neighbors, if you offer them too many opportunities for easy living. Raccoons will build dens in sheds and outbuildings, under porches, and in woodpiles. They like to forage in garbage cans, at pet-food bowls, and at bird feeders. They will enter homes through pet doors and unlatched screen doors in search of food and water. Raccoons often find bird baths, livestock troughs, and drip irrigation convenient sources of water.

Ridding yourself of unwanted raccoons will require that you remove these attractions from your property. Close off entrances to sheds and porches to keep raccoons out. Garbage can lids must fit tightly and be weighted. The cans should be stored in a rack or tied down to prevent being tipped over. Pet food should be kept indoors at night. Try feeding pets only enough food for one meal, and avoid leaving extra food for raccoons. Latch pet doors and screen doors at night. Eliminate unnecessary open water or keep it fenced in. An occasional visit by raccoons passing through your yard can be delightful. The trick is to enjoy raccoons without giving them the opportunity to alter their natural lifestyle.

BACKYARD MAMMALS

Ringtail
Bassariscus astutus

Characteristics::
A medium-sized, grayish mammal with a long, slender body; tail long with alternating black and white rings; whitish ring around black eyes; no facial mask.

Ringtails are residents of rocky slopes and canyon walls throughout our range. They nest in mine tunnels, in caves, in rock crevices, among boulders and in buildings. Other names for the ringtail include civetcat, ring-tailed cat,

59

miner's cat and coon-cat. These names describe the ringtail's catlike grace and appearance, but they are not cats at all. Ringtails are members of the raccoon family.

Ringtails are strictly nocturnal, often covering several miles each night while hunting for mice, rabbits, lizards, snakes and insects. They also eat the fruit of cacti and other plants. In defensive situations, a ringtail will excrete a foul-smelling fluid from its anal gland. This probably acts to repel predators, such as great-horned owls and bobcats.

Ringtails are agile climbers and move easily on steep rocky terrain. They are powerful and accurate jumpers. By rotating their feet 180 degrees, they can climb and descend very steep surfaces. This adaptation also allows a ringtail to reverse directions on a narrow ledge.

Undeterred by human presence, ringtails are notorious for stealing campers' food. They will take up residence in attics and outbuildings. They also find good hunting for mice and other prey around the edges of developed areas. For problems with ringtails, follow the techniques described in the section on raccoons (pg. 56-58).

Striped Skunk
Mephitis mephitis

Characteristics:
A mammal the size of a domestic cat; bushy tail; black with two broad, white stripes on back; stripes merge at shoulders; thin white stripe on forehead.

Striped skunks live throughout most of the United States and are common in the central Arizona uplands. They live in all of our vegetation types. Skunks create dens in the natural cavities between rocks and boulders. They also use burrows dug by foxes and badgers, and will enlarge bur-

rows dug by ground squirrels and other rodents to a size large enough accommodate them.

Striped skunks, typically, have two distinct white stripes starting at the back of the head or shoulder and continuing to the tip of the tail. The skunks in our area often have such wide stripes that they run together and appear as a single white band. This makes it difficult to separate the striped skunk from the less common hooded skunk (*Mephitis macroura*) which also lives in our area. The hooded skunk has a single, white band on its back. To be certain of which skunk you are viewing, look closely for a thin white stripe extending from the base of the ears, along the sides, to the front thighs. This lateral stripe is characteristic of the hooded skunk and is absent on the striped skunk.

Striped skunks are omnivorous, but most of their diet (70%) consists of animal foods. They eat insects, small mammals, bird eggs, berries and other plant material. Striped skunks prefer beetles, grasshoppers and crickets, when available.

Striped skunks are bold yet gentle creatures. They amble about without haste or regard for their concealment. They go where they please with little fear of danger, and they are rarely aggressive. Perhaps the striped skunk's self-confident demeanor and nonaggressive behavior are the result of its most effective defense—the ability to spray a discharge of potent musk at an attacker. When agitated a striped skunk will elevate its tail and stomp its front feet. If sufficiently threatened, it will arch its back, aim its rear-end, and discharge musk from its specially adapted anal glands. Striped skunks can control the discharge and release it as either a fine atomized mist or as a concentrated spray. The droplets of the atomized mist are so fine that the discharge looks like a cloud of steam. If the skunk chooses to spray in a concentrated form, it can accurately project the spray up to fifteen feet. The overwhelming smell of the musk is nauseating and will temporarily depress a victim's central nervous system. The lingering smell of the musk can last for weeks and is very difficult to wash off. Because of its tenacious qualities, the musk is used as a perfume base. If you or a pet have been sprayed by a skunk, try washing with liberal amounts of vinegar or tomato juice. This will help reduce the odor, but only time will remove it completely. Wash clothes and other objects with bleach, ammonia or carbolic soap.

Striped skunks are solitary animals except during mating and when rearing their young. Mating occurs in late winter, and the female bears four to eleven young in April or May. The kits arrive with their white and black pattern in place. They begin producing musk in about two weeks, and their eyes open about one week later. By two months of age the young are fending for themselves. In late autumn, the kits set out on their own. In the central Arizona uplands, unlike areas with colder climates, striped skunks remain active all year. They are primarily nocturnal and spend the daytime nestled in the comfort of a den.

There is no need to fear skunks in your backyard unless they have taken up residence under your house, or you own a dog that likes to chase animals. If you keep a reasonable distance, it is unlikely that you will get sprayed. Skunks are reluctant to foul themselves with musk, unless they are truly in danger. Skunks are highly susceptible to rabies. **If you come across a sick or aggressive skunk, particularly if it is active during the day, give it a wide berth.** Keep your pets restrained, and call your local animal control office or the Arizona Game and Fish Department immediately.

If you have a problem with a skunk living under your house, you must find the point of entry and close it off. To ensure that the skunk has left before you close off the entrance, try the following method. First prepare the boards, wire mesh, or other materials that you will need to close off the hole. To prevent skunks from digging under your repairs, bury wire mesh against the foundation and extending away from the house at a ninety-degree angle. If there is more than one entryway, close off all but the largest and most obvious one. Then clear the area in front of the entrance of leaves, pine needles or other vegetation, so that you have bare soil. Work around any plants, rocks or other obstacles that you are unable to remove. Then smooth out the soil and sprinkle a thin coat of white baking flour on the bare ground. Leave the area undisturbed until about one hour after dark. Hopefully, when you return you will find the tracks left by the skunk's exit. Look closely with the beam of a flashlight held parallel to the ground. Be sure the tracks lead only away from the hole. Now close off the entrance. Don't worry about your evicted tenants, they will probably find a new place to den by morning.

BACKYARD MAMMALS

Javelina
Tayassu tajacu

Characteristics:
A medium-sized, piglike mammal; bristly hair is dark brown to black with white tips; white collar in winter.

Javelina, also called collared peccary, are native to South and Central America, Mexico and the southwestern United States. In Arizona, javelina live throughout the southern and central part of the state. Their range is naturally expanding northward. Javelina are recent inhabitants of the central Arizona uplands and have become com-

mon here only in the past twenty or thirty years. Javelina are residents of the grasslands, chaparral and woodlands. In the summer, they are also present in the pine forests. They are becoming more frequent in and around towns and cities. Javelina live in areas with dense vegetation, rock crevices, caves, boulder piles and mine shafts.

Javelina are only distantly related to domestic pigs. They are members of the peccary family which contains two other similar animals that live in South and Central America. Javelina eat cactus, agave, bulbs, tubers, acorns, juniper berries, mesquite beans, grasses and herbs. Prickly pear cactus make up a large portion of the javelina's diet. They eat the spines, fruit and pads without hesitation or injury. Where surface water is limited, cactus pads provide a portion of javelina's water needs.

To avoid the daytime heat during the summer, javelina are active only at night. In the fall and winter, they are active throughout the day and the night with occasional resting periods interspersed. Urban javelina tend to remain nocturnal throughout the year.

Javelina's bristly coats are brownish-black or dark gray and flecked with white. In the winter they have a distinct white collar about their shoulders. During the warmer months, javelina molt and their coats become thinner and lighter in color as the hair falls away. The thinner coat helps them stay cool by reducing insulation, and its lighter color reflects the heat of the summer sun.

Javelina's eyes are not designed for distant viewing. Only objects that are within two to three feet are clearly focused. They can see objects up to 100 yards away, but the detection of such poorly focused images is dependent on their movement. What javelina lack in eyesight, they make up for with a tremendously acute sense of smell. They use it to detect predators, to identify one another, and to locate food. By smell alone, javelina can find bulbs, roots and tubers buried beneath several inches of soil.

Like most cloven-hoofed animals, javelina have a well-developed scent gland. Located just above the tail, the scent gland produces an oily musk. Javelina use the gland to identify one another, to keep the herd together, and to mark their territories. The strong musk is sometimes noticeable to the human nose. Javelina forage in small herds. As the herd moves about, they stay together by following each other's scent with their keen noses. During windy conditions the herd cohesion often becomes difficult to maintain and individuals become easily separated.

Javelina are social animals that live in tightly knit herds of three to thirty individuals. Herds include family members of many ages and of both sexes. A strong bond is maintained among herd members with close contact during bedding, feeding and play. Individual bonds are strengthened by an activity called reciprocal rubbing. During this behavior, two javelina vigorously rub the sides of their heads against one another's scent glands.

Javelina breed and have young throughout the year, although breeding activity peaks during the fall and winter. Sows give birth in the herd's bedding area, which is centrally located within its territory. Litters range from two to four piglings. The piglings are reddish-brown and have a dark stripe on the back, from the snout to the tail. At two to three months of age, the young javelina's coloration begins to darken to that of the adult. Bobcats, coyotes and foxes prey on the vulnerable young javelina and black bears and mountain lions prey on the adults.

Javelina are becoming increasingly common in and around developed areas. Here they find it easy to meet the essential needs of food, shelter and water. Pet food, bird seed, garbage, fruit from horticultural trees, flower beds and vegetable gardens provide javelina with an abundant source of food. Javelina find shelter in culverts, in crawl spaces, and under bridges and mobile homes. In cities water is always nearby and javelina are safe from most predators, including human hunters. The growing urban javelina populations are becoming a serious problem for residents. Javelina dig up gardens and flower beds when searching for food. They reside under homes and occasionally injure dogs that are foolish enough to chase them. Some residents fear that javelina may actually attack them. Although there are very few documented cases of javelina actually injuring people, the risk is increasing as javelina continue to populate urban areas.

Human population growth in central Arizona has increased dramatically over the past several decades. As our communities grow, so does the potential for javelina to make an easy living. As a result, unnaturally large javelina populations are living in our towns, cities and rural areas. The way to reduce javelina problems is to limit their access to food, water and shelter.

Don't feed javelina. By doing so, you disturb their natural foraging behavior and encourage them into your neighborhood where they create problems for others. Place bird feeders a minimum of four feet from the ground and don't allow spilled seed to accumulate. You may want to keep feeders within fenced areas to limit access entirely. Don't discard edible garbage where javelina can get to it. If you feed your pets outdoors, do not allow excess food to be left out for prolonged periods. Pick up fruit from trees as it drops to the ground, before it attracts javelina. Try landscaping with plants other than those that javelina eat. Avoid using cactus and other succulent plants. Plants with bulbs and tubers and trees or shrubs with abundant fruit or nuts also attract javelina. Turn pails, tubs, pet food dishes and other containers upside down so they don't collect rain water. Fill depressions that might puddle from rain or from irrigation systems.

If javelina are eating plants in your garden, fencing is your only option. Fencing does not need to be elaborate or expensive. Javelina can't jump very high, if at all, and any well-constructed fence that is at least three feet tall and strong enough to resist being pushed over easily will do the job. Low-voltage electric fencing is inexpensive and very effective in keeping out javelina. Powered by two "D" batteries, these fences are safe and economical to operate. A single wire strand placed ten inches above the ground and encircling the area will do the job. The cost to fence a 25-by-25 foot area with a low-voltage electric fence is about $100. Materials can be purchased at ranch- supply and fencing stores. This type of fencing is not visually obtrusive and may be acceptable in housing developments with strict fencing rules.

Other techniques to ward off unwanted javelina include spreading cayenne pepper around feeding areas, placing ammonia-soaked rags in frequented areas, and spreading a mixture of glycerine and lion, tiger, or other big-cat feces around your yard. You can get the cat feces from zoos.

It is very unlikely that javelina will attack a person unless they are threatened or cornered. But if necessary, javelina are capable of defending themselves and are equipped with large canine teeth to do so. If you find a javelina trapped within a fenced area, open the gate and allow it to leave on its own. Trying to chase it out may become dangerous. When startled, a javelina will often take a couple of steps forward before turning and running away. This behavior may appear to be aggressive, but it is more likely an attempt to get a closer look with its poor eyesight. Or this may be a technique to intimidate a potential predator.

Javelina usually avoid encounters with people, but in some urban areas they have become desensitized and may linger about. If you don't want javelina in your yard, spray them with a hose; yell at them; throw rocks and in general make your yard an unpleasant place for them to visit.

Mule Deer
Odocoileus hemionus

Characteristics:
A large cloven-hoofed mammal; large mule-like ears; narrow rope-like tail; male have branching antlers with two thick beams.

Mule deer are common throughout the central Arizona uplands. They live in the forest, woodlands, chaparral, and riparian areas. The mule deer's diet varies with the

seasons. They eat grasses and herbaceous plants in the warmer months, and the foliage of trees and shrubs in the fall and winter.

Mule deer are most active in the early morning and during the late afternoon. They spend the rest of the day bedded down under the cover of trees and shrubs. An opportunity to watch these graceful creatures is always a delight. Next time you startle a mule deer on the roadside or in your yard, look closely at how all four hoofs leave the ground at one time. This stiff-legged, bounding movement is called "stotting." Stotting is thought to show the fleeing animal's good health and vigor . This display of fitness signals a potential predator that it is fit and not worth chasing.

The male deer grows antlers from early spring through midwinter. When the antlers are fully developed, they become a symbol of a buck's strength and vitality. The antlers play an important role in determining a buck's social standing within the herd and subsequently, its success at breeding. In late spring the antlers are shed and by early summer a new set begins to grow.

In December and January, during a period called "the rut," male mule deer compete for females. Younger or smaller bucks challenge the dominant males for access to a group of females. Competitive techniques include snorting, thrashing of heads and gestures of intimidation. Some mule deer competitions result in antler-locking duels. A ruling male defends his harem from other challengers while he mates with each of the receptive females. From July through September, the female mule deer gives birth to one or two young. The fawns are born with white spots that help them blend into the colors and patterns of their surroundings. The newborn deer remain hidden in the brush for the first three or four days. After that, they follow the mother as she forages with the herd.

People enjoy seeing deer in the backyard, but they can cause considerable damage by eating vegetable gardens, flowers, and ornamental trees and shrubs. Chemical repellents applied directly to leaves and flowers are effective for deterring deer. These products are available at most garden centers, but are safe only for inedible plants. Other techniques for repelling deer include hanging shiny objects such as strips of tinfoil or mirrors around the property and hanging nylon stockings that contain bits of human hair. Scarecrows and wind-generated noisemakers may also be effective. Deer are adaptable and will soon adjust to most repellents. Regularly changing the position of your repellents may prolong their effectiveness. The only permanent solution for a deer problem is to fence them out. Mule deer are skilled jumpers and fencing must be at least six feet high to keep them from leaping over it.

BACKYARD MAMMALS

Pronghorn
Antilocapra americana

Characteristics:
A large golden-brown, cloven-hoofed mammal; white rump, neck and underparts; horns curve back and inward at tips; males have prongs midway on horns.

Pronghorn live in the grasslands of valleys and mesa tops. They prefer flat, open areas where they can see long distances and run at high speeds. Pronghorn herds, con-

taining hundreds of individuals, once roamed Arizona's grasslands, but their numbers have been greatly reduced by hunting, grazing competition from livestock, and habitat loss. Small herds of pronghorn are scattered throughout the central Arizona uplands. The largest herd is about 400 individuals and lives on the Fain Ranch, east of Prescott Valley.

The commonly used names of "antelope" and "pronghorn antelope" are misnomers for this species. Pronghorn are unique to North America and are not at all related to the true antelope of Africa and Eurasia. Pronghorn are the only member of the family *Antilocapridae.* Their horn structure consisting of a bony interior and a hornlike sheath is one of the characteristics that make the pronghorn unique. Early each winter, both the males and the females shed the outer sheaths of their horns. A new sheath immediately begins to grow and is fully developed by the middle of the next summer.

Pronghorn are the fastest land animals in North America and can run at speeds in excess of sixty miles per hour. They have very large eyes and can see great distances. A pronghorn's two-inch-diameter eyes are comparable, in size, to those of an elephant. Their speed and long-distance vision make healthy adult pronghorn very difficult to capture, though curiosity will often bring them closer to a human hunter. Mountain lions prey on adult pronghorn, and the vulnerable newborn are frequently killed by coyotes.

In the spring and summer pronghorn separate into herds of males and herds of females with juveniles. In the fall males establish and defend territories. Mating occurs when the female herds move through the territories of the males. After the mating season, males abandon their territories and once again form all-male herds. Females give birth to one or two young in the spring. For the first several days of its life, a newborn pronghorn lies almost motionless while it gains the strength to stand. During this time the mother stays nearby to defend it from predators. By three weeks of age, young pronghorn are strong enough to outrun most predators. At this time, the mother and fawn join a nursing herd where the young quickly mature.

The traditional home ranges of pronghorn are becoming smaller as more homes, businesses and roads are constructed in grassland areas such as Prescott Valley. Pronghorn naturally move about from one area to another in response to changes in weather, forage conditions and availability of water. Encroaching development restricts pronghorn movement and isolates herds from one another. It can also reduce herd size by decreasing the amount of land that is available to support the population.

Unlike deer and elk, pronghorn will not jump fences. They will either crawl under a fence, or follow along it in search of a place to pass through. Many barbed-wire fences have been converted by ranchers and land managers to a type that allows pronghorn to crawl under. The bottom strand of these fences is barbless and raised to eighteen inches above the ground. Pronghorn will cross a road if it is not fenced on both sides. Crawling under both fences and dodging traffic seems to be too great a risk for pronghorn.

Community planning efforts to help pronghorn survive must create travel corridors and maintain grasslands. This is critical for the future well-being of this remarkable species.

Backyard BIRDS

BACKYARD BIRDS

American Kestrel
Falco sparverius

Characteristics:
A small falcon; rufous back and tail, double black mustache; males have blue-gray wings.

American kestrels are common summer residents in the central Arizona uplands. They frequent open areas such as grasslands, parks and woodlands that have a few trees for perching and nesting. Kestrels are the smallest of the

falcons and are only about the size of mourning doves. They hunt for insects, lizards and small birds by hovering and pouncing, or by dropping on them from a perch. Their favorite perches include power lines, telephone poles and fences.

American kestrels nest in natural hollows in trees and in cavities that were excavated by woodpeckers such as northern flickers. Their courtship and nesting displays may last for several weeks and include extended periods of noisy vocalizations. When nest cavities are scarce, kestrels will force other birds from their holes and take over occupancy.

In the winter male and female American kestrels move to different habitats where they are solitary until spring. The males prefer the denser and more forested or shrubby areas in the northern part of the winter range. The females prefer the open areas such as desert grasslands in the southern part of the winter range. The reason for the different habitat use is unclear, but it may have something to do with prey abundance, prey size, the hunting techniques used by each sex, or a combination of several of these factors.

A falcon silhouette placed on large windows will help keep yardbirds from crashing into the glass as they attempt to fly through "gaps" that windows seem to represent to them.

BACKYARD BIRDS

Gambel's Quail
Callipepla gambelii

Characteristics:
A small, chickenlike, game bird; grayish body; black plume on head; chestnut crown; black spot in buff patch on belly of male; female head coloration is drab.

Gambel's quail are common year-round residents in the grasslands and chaparral of our region. They spend most of their time on the ground in search of seeds, tender leaves, fruits and legumes. Gambel's quail live in flocks,

or coveys, averaging twenty to thirty birds, but coveys of 100 or more individuals are not uncommon. They are common yardbirds when sufficient natural habitat is available in a neighborhood.

Female Gambel's quail lay ten to twelve eggs in a shallow scrape in the ground lined with soft vegetation such as grass, leaves or twigs. The quail's large clutch size helps to combat the increased danger of predation caused by nesting on the ground. Eggs and young are preyed upon by snakes, squirrels, ants, roadrunners and domestic cats and dogs. Hawks and raptors also prey on adult Gambel's quail. Gambel's quail are one of the most popular game animals in Arizona and sportsmen harvest thousands each year.

Quail reproduction is closely linked to the amount of rainfall each year. In wet years quail populations boom, but in dry years their numbers are suppressed by the lack of forage and by a unique chemical relationship to the plants they feed upon. In dry years, many plants, especially those in the pea family, produce high quantities of a chemical compound that mimics quail reproductive hormones. The increased concentration of these chemical compounds decreases quail reproductive success and may serve to protect the plants from over-consumption during dry years.

BACKYARD BIRDS

Mourning Dove
Zenaida macroura

Characteristics:
A medium-sized bird: brownish-gray; pointed tail has white edges; black spots on upper wings.

Mourning doves are familiar residents of urban areas throughout most of the United States. In the wild, they live from the low deserts to the high mountain forests. Mourn-

83

ing doves are easily recognized by their streamlined appearance and the whistling sound of their wings when they take flight.

The name "mourning dove" is derived from the birds' melancholy song. Ninety-nine percent of a mourning dove's diet is made up of seeds. An occasional bit of greenery or a few insects make up the remaining one percent of their diet. Mourning doves are fond of cultivated grains and are common in farm fields and at bird feeders. And like the Gambel's quail, they are a very popular game species.

During courtship the male mourning dove performs a series of graceful flights in curves, arches and spirals. The female dove watches from a nearby perch, and if she is sufficiently impressed, a pair bond is established. The mourning-dove pair bond often lasts for several years. Male doves collect the nesting materials while females construct a shallow saucer-shaped platform in the fork of a tree or on the ground. Each clutch contains two or three eggs, and mourning doves commonly have two or three clutches each year. The male dove incubates the eggs during most of the day, and the female sits on the eggs the remainder of the day and all through the night. The eggs hatch in thirteen or fourteen days. The young develop rapidly and are fully feathered and capable of flying in about two weeks.

Barn Owl
Tyto alba

Characteristics:
A large owl; whitish underparts, rusty back, white heart-shaped facial disk; no ear tufts.

Barn owls are found in the lower elevations of our region. Their ghostly appearance and raspy, hissing voice adds to the reputation of owls as mysterious creatures of

the night.

Barn owls hunt for rodents in the open spaces of grasslands, farms, and woodlands. They also can be found in rocky canyons and agricultural areas which attract mice and other rodents.

With their keen eyes, unique ears and silent flight, barn owls are especially adapted to their night time world. Their eyes reflect and reabsorb light, doubling illumination and enhancing night vision. They have seven times as many rods and cones as human eyes, and can see approximately fifty times clearer than humans can in low-light situations. The two ears of a barn owl are each at a different height and have different shapes. This allows an owl to triangulate the location of a sound with great accuracy. Like most owls, barn owls have specially adapted flight feathers that have a loose fringe along the leading edge. This fringe divides the air currents that strike the wing during flight and allows the barn owl to fly without making a sound. With these remarkable adaptations, barn owls can catch mice in total darkness.

Barn owls nest in caves, in mine tunnels, on cliff ledges, in hollow trees, in old buildings, in barns, and in stacks of baled hay. If you have barn owls in your attic, barn, or outbuilding, think twice before you evict them. They are probably helping to keep the local rodent populations in check. If you choose to close off access to a barn owl nest or roost area, place a wooden nest box nearby. Barn owls easily adapt to nest boxes, and many people have been successful at relocating them.

Hummingbirds
Family: Trochilidae

Characteristics:
Tiny birds with long, needle-like bills and hovering flight; iridescent feathers on head and throat of males; females drab-green; both sexes mostly green above.

Hummingbirds are one of nature's most spectacular gems. In the central Arizona uplands, we are fortunate to have several species living here during the summer months. They occur in all of our vegetation types, but are most often seen in riparian areas. Our most common hummingbirds include the Anna's (*Calypte anna*), black-chinned (*Archilochus alexandri*), and broad-tailed (*Selasphorus platycercus*) species.

Hummingbirds eat flower nectar and insects. They fly by quickly beating the entire wing without flexing it at the elbow or wrist. This unique flight method allows hummingbirds to fly forward, backward and to hover with great control and accuracy. Their rapid

wingbeats occur at 80-200 beats per second.

There are many unique attributes that set hummers apart from other birds. Hummingbirds have the most dense plumage, yet the smallest number of feathers of any birds. They consume more than twice their body weight in food and more than eight times their body weight in water each day. Hummingbirds are the smallest of all warm-blooded animals. They also have the fastest heart rate of warm-blooded animals (1260 beats per minute). Because of this, their muscles, hearts and brains are proportionately larger than those of any other birds.

You can attract hummingbirds by landscaping with brightly colored flowering shrubs and wildflowers. Hummingbirds particularly like plants with tubular flowers. Some of these include penstemon, Indian paintbrush, honeysuckle, skyrocket and columbine. Nectar feeders are also an effective way to attract hummingbirds to your yard. A solution of one cup of table sugar to four or five cups of water is a good ratio for matching the natural nectar of flowers. Never use sugar substitutes. They have little or no nutritional value. Honey is also not recommended because it spoils quickly and the fungus which it grows can be lethal to the birds. Be sure to clean your feeders at least once a week with hot water and a drop of vinegar to kill any molds. Keeping fresh nectar in your feeders is important for the health of your hummingbird visitors.

Enjoy feeding the hummingbirds during the spring and summer, but take your feeder down during the colder months. The unnaturally abundant food supply provided by your feeder may interfere with hummingbirds' natural cues for the start of winter migration.

BACKYARD BIRDS

Northern Flicker
Colaptes auratus

Characteristics:
A medium-sized woodpecker; barred brown back, spotted white belly, white rump, orange underwings; male has red moustache.

Northern flickers are common in the woodlands and pine forests of the central Arizona uplands. They hunt for insects under the bark of trees and on the ground. Ants are one of their favorite prey. They also eat berries, nuts and seeds in the winter when insects are less abundant. The northern flicker in our area is of the "red-shafted" color variation and has red-orange under the wings.

By drilling nesting cavities in trees, flickers play an important role in the forest and woodland. After the flickers abandon these holes, they

89

provide shelter for a large number of bird species, including bluebirds, American kestrels, flammulated owls and mountain chickadees. Many of these birds are dependent on flicker and other woodpecker holes for nesting cavities.

Northern flickers sometimes drill nest holes in the wooden siding of houses. This is not only destructive, but also creates a tremendous amount of racket for the residents. The most important factors in successfully deterring flickers from pecking holes in your siding is your early detection and swift actions. Flickers (and other woodpeckers) will become progressively more difficult to drive away as time passes without disruption of their construction efforts. Metal sheeting over pecked areas is a good deterrent, but may just cause the bird to begin a new hole. Try rubbing linseed oil on the pecked surfaces. Wind-powered motion devices such as toy pinwheels, aluminum-foil strips or pie pans suspended from strings may repel the woodpeckers. Or you may be able to redirect the pecking to a bird box (without a hole) placed over the pecked area. In this case you will still need to put up with several days of hammering, but it will keep the birds from ruining your siding. If these techniques fail, seek the help of a licensed wildlife-service company that is authorized to set traps to capture the birds and deploy chemical repellents.

BACKYARD BIRDS

Acorn Woodpecker
Melanerpes formicivorus

Characteristics:
A medium-sized woodpecker; black wings, back, tail and chest; red crown; white eyes; white facial pattern.

Acorn woodpeckers are year-round residents of the woodlands and forests of the central Arizona uplands. They are commonly found in and around developed areas with oak trees and shrubs. Acorn woodpeckers eat insects, acorns, fruit and tree sap. They nest in the natural cavities of larger pine and oak trees.

Acorn woodpeckers live in family groups of up to sixteen members. Each family collects, stores and defends a hoard of acorns for the fall and winter. The acorns are jammed into shallow holes that they drill into dead, standing trees. These trees, sometimes called granaries, become riddled with holes as thousands of acorns are cached. The acorns are hammered so tightly into the holes, it is difficult for potential robbers to steal them. Acorn woodpeckers are often seen chasing squirrels, jays, nuthatches and other woodpeckers in defense of their granaries.

Telephone poles and sign posts are sometimes converted to granaries by acorn woodpeckers. The shallow holes usually do not weaken the pole or post, but may damage its appearance. If you wish to stop the drilling by acorn woodpeckers try painting the pole with linseed oil or one of the nonlethal bird-repellent products such as *Hot Foot* or *Bird Be Gone*. These products are available at most hardware stores and garden centers.

BACKYARD BIRDS

Scrub Jay
Aphelocoma coerulescens

Characteristics:
A medium-sized bird; blue tail, rump and head; pale brown upper back; light-grey chest; sexes are similar.

This bright-blue jay is a common year-round resident throughout our area. Its gregarious behavior and loud "check-check-check-check" vocalizations are typical in

urban areas with pinyon pines, junipers, oaks, and along riparian areas. Scrub jays are natural inhabitants of woodlands and the transitional areas between woodlands and pine forests, and woodlands and chaparral. They are often seen combing the trees in pairs, or in small groups, looking for insects, small lizards, nuts, seeds or fruits. Scrub jays have a taste for the eggs and young of other birds. During the spring and summer they commonly rob the nests of other songbirds. During the fall and winter months, when animal foods are less common, they feed primarily on acorns, pinyon nuts and other fruits and seeds. Some of these foods are pirated from the stores of packrats and acorn woodpeckers. Scrub jays store food themselves by burying it in the dirt and duff, and by wedging it into the cracks and crevices of rocky areas. Forgotten scrub jay-food caches probably make a significant contribution to the propagation of pinyon pines, junipers and oaks.

Scrub jays can be a nuisance at bird feeders. Quite often they dominate the food supply and chase other birds away. One method to keep them from controlling the bird food is to use a specially designed feeder that closes under the weight of larger birds. This is not always foolproof, but it will work for awhile. If you want to attract scrub jays, try raking up small piles of acorns beneath the trees that produced them, or collect them from neighboring areas. Scrub jays love a good bath and are easily attracted to birdbaths. Perhaps the best way to attract scrub jays is to plant pinyon pines and native oak trees in your landscaping.

BACKYARD BIRDS

Common Raven
Corvus corax

Characteristics:
A large, all-black songbird; large, thick bill; wedge-shaped tail; shaggy throat feathers.

The common raven can be found throughout the central Arizona uplands, but they are more abundant in mountains and canyons. Ravens are hawklike in their flying and soaring behavior, but in good light, they are quickly distinguished from most birds of prey by their jet-black plumage.

Ravens eat carrion, lizards, bird eggs, nestlings, insects, garbage, seeds and fruit. They frequently cache food for a short period of time, and like hawks and owls, eject indigestible items such as bones and fur in a pellet. Ravens build large stick nests on rock ledges or in tall coniferous trees. They frequently repair the nest and use it from year to year. In the nest, the female lays from four to six eggs and rears two to four young each year.

This gregarious and highly vocal bird is the largest member of the songbird (passerine) family. They have a reputation for being very intelligent, and captive birds have learned to open cages, perform for food, and count. One classic example of animal tool use is that of ravens dropping rocks on climbers as they approach from below.

Ravens actively engage in play. They pull each other's tails, pass stones back and forth, and offer sticks to each other, then jerk them away in a teasing manner. They also play together by wheeling and tumbling in flight. Their vocabulary is very large, and some of their calls have as many as five syllables. The "kaaa" call of an adult raven signals danger and alerts other ravens. The "kukuk" call is a location call and is usually given in flight, while the "krackkrackkrackkrack" call is an invitation to other ravens to "come fly." Ravens also communicate nonverbally with a wide array of body postures.

BACKYARD BIRDS

American Robin
Turdus migratorius

Characteristics:
A medium-sized songbird; dark-gray back and head; burnt-orange breast; dark stripes on white throat.

The American robin is perhaps the best-known songbird in North America. Common in towns and cities, it occurs throughout central Arizona. Many consider the robin's rich, melodic song the first sign of spring. Perhaps it was the hope of spring that led to the robin's song being described as "cheer-up cheerily." Robins eat earthworms, snails, fruit and insects. They build cuplike nests of twigs

and mud in trees and shrubs and on the ledges of buildings.

A robin hunts for earthworms by standing motionless with its head turned to one side. This posture gives the appearance that the bird is listening for the worm. It is actually looking for it and must cock its head to get a good view with its monocular vision.

Robins were once the victims of a toxic agricultural chemical called DDT. During the 1950s and '60s, DDT was used in many urban areas to control Dutch elm disease. The leaves of elm trees were coated with the chemical to combat the disease. These leaves then fell to the ground and were consumed by earthworms. The worms concentrated the DDT and stored it in their bodies. When robins ate the earthworms, they either died outright or suffered reproductive failure. DDT has been banned in the United States since 1972. Since then robin populations have rebounded and they continue to delight us with their cheery songs of spring. Unfortunately, DDT is still used liberally in other countries that fall within the winter range of robins and many other migratory songbirds. This, combined with the loss of breeding habitat, wintering grounds and migration corridors, is having a tragic impact on our migratory songbirds.

European Starling
Sturnus vulgaris

Characteristics:
A medium-small songbird; spring plumage is black with iridescent green and purple; winter plumage is dull black-brown with light spots; bill is yellow in spring and dark in fall.

The European starling is an introduced species common throughout the continental United States. Its native home is Europe and Asia. In 1890, sixty European starlings were introduced into New York City's Central Park. Starling numbers increased rapidly as they pushed their

way west across the continent. The first record of starlings in Arizona dates from 1946; by 1950 they had reached the West Coast.

Starlings have been associated with humans since the invention of agriculture. They make a comfortable living from the fruits and seeds of cultivated plants and the insects they attract. Starlings are most commonly found in flocks of ten to fifty birds, but flocks sometimes reach several hundred individuals. These large flocks can severely damage agricultural crops. Starlings evade the attacks of hawks and falcons by flying together in aerial maneuvers of wheeling, twisting flight. They also confuse predators by expanding and contracting the flock as they fly.

Starlings are secondary cavity nesters, which means that they don't construct their own nesting holes. They use the holes made by woodpeckers or find cracks and crevices in buildings. Their gregarious behavior and prodigious reproduction give starlings an advantage over many native species. Starlings out-compete bluebirds, titmice, chickadees and other cavity-nesting birds for a place to nest. In this way, they keep the other species from successfully reproducing.

There are a variety of methods for ridding an area of starlings. Unfortunately, all of these methods are temporary at best. The only real solution for a starling problem is to exclude them from critical areas such as gardens or fruit trees. A fine mesh netting can be draped over fruit trees and staked to the ground or suspended over a garden fence. Netting of this sort is available at most garden centers and some hardware stores. Starlings are one of the few birds that are not protected by the Migratory Bird Treaty and do not require a federal permit for destruction. If you have a starling problem that might warrant killing the birds, contact the Arizona Game and Fish Department for advice on safe and effective methods before proceeding.

BACKYARD BIRDS

House Finch
Carpodacus mexicanus

Characteristics:
A small songbird; male has bright-red breast, forehead, eyeline and rump; dark stripes on light belly; dark wings and tail. Female is brownish-gray, striped and lacks red.

House finches are year-round residents throughout the central Arizona uplands. In the winter they are more common in the lower elevations where it is warmer. Another less common name for the house finch is the "linnet," after a somewhat similar European species.

As their name suggests, house finches do well in urban areas. They nest under the eaves of buildings, in trees and shrubs, and in nests built by other species. The house finch's strong, wide bill is well adapted for cracking the tough hulls of seeds. Their diet is comprised almost exclusively of the seeds of grasses, shrubs and other plants. They occasionally eat fruit and buds. You can easily encourage them by planting sunflowers. The house finch's song is an undulating series of bright notes.

House finches are one of the most common bird species at feeders in our area, and their range is thought to be expanding as a result of this supplemental feeding. They roost in large numbers under the foliage of vines during the winter and occasionally nest there.

BACKYARD BIRDS

House Sparrow
Passer domesticus

Characteristics:
A small songbird; male has black throat, white cheeks and brown nape; female is dull-gray with buffy eyeline.

The house sparrow is a native of Europe and is now abundant throughout most of the world. House sparrows were first introduced into North America in the mid-1800s for their aesthetic beauty and to control insect pests. Like

the starling, they spread quickly to colonize all of the United States and much of Canada. The first house sparrows reached Arizona in the early 1900s. They came by moving west along the railroad corridors, feeding on spilt grain. Other house sparrows traveled west aboard the trains after being trapped within the cars.

In the early 1900s, house sparrows were the most abundant bird species in the U.S. Their large populations were supported by the grain fed to horses and by the insects found in the horse manure. With the invention of the automobile, sparrow populations decreased as horses became a secondary mode of transportation. House sparrows are still very abundant near farms and feed lots and in urban areas.

House sparrows eat a varied diet of seeds, fruit, insects and spiders. They build spherical nests under the eaves of buildings, in natural cavities of trees, or in the dense foliage of trees and shrubs. House sparrows often forcibly appropriate the nests of other birds and sometimes destroy the eggs and young of the other birds in the process. For this reason, they are a threat to some native bird species and are not protected by state and federal laws, as most birds are.

To prevent house sparrows from nesting under the eaves of your home, cover openings with plywood or wire-mesh screen and tear down old nests which are frequently reused. Placing slanted metal or wooden boards on ledges at an angle of forty-five degrees or more will prevent sparrows from perching there. Scare devices such as rubber snakes and owl statues are sometimes effective at repelling sparrows, but they must be placed in appropriate places and be moved frequently.

*B*ackyard
REPTILES

BACKYARD REPTILES

Lizards
Iguanidae, Scincidae, Teiidae Families

Characteristics:
Four-legged, scaled reptiles; toes clawed; eyelids moveable; most have long tails.

The central Arizona uplands are home to many species of lizards. They live in all of our vegetation types and vary greatly in their size, coloration, habitat and behavior. Some of the more common lizards include the tree lizard (*Urosaurus ornatus*), the eastern fence lizard (*Sceloporus undulatus*), the short-horned lizard (*Phrynosoma douglassi*), the western whiptail (*Cnemidophorus tigris*), and the many-lined skink (*Eumeces multivirgatus*).

short-horned lizard

Most of the lizards found in the central Arizona uplands are active during the day when temperatures are high enough to heat up their cold-blooded metabolism. Lizards eat ants, spiders, termites, insects, ticks, millipedes and scorpions. They are prey to a wide variety of birds, mammals and a few snakes.

tree lizard

Male lizards perform territorial and courtship displays by bobbing up and down in what appear to be pushups. These social displays are an attempt to chase another male out of its territory or to display its strength and vigor to a female.

Lizards avoid predators in a variety of ways. Some species such as the short-horned and eastern fence lizards have patterns and colors that make them nearly impossible to see against the natural background. Whiptail lizards escape by speeding away along predetermined runways. In another survival mode, several species can puff themselves up when inside a crack. This makes it nearly impossible to pry them loose. Almost all lizards can escape a close call by shedding their tails. The wriggling tail leaves predators confused as the

many-lined skink

108

lizard escapes to safety. The lizard's tail grows back in a matter of weeks.

Most lizard young are born from eggs in underground burrows. One exception to this is the short-horned lizard, which bears live young. Some species of whiptail lizards consist of only females. They reproduce without mating in a fascinating, asexual process called parthenogenesis. As a result of this reproductive process, all of the offspring are genetically identical to one another and to their mother.

Lizards are one of the more watchable wildlife species in the central Arizona uplands. Unfortunately, they are the victims of severe predation by domestic cats. Protect lizards from your cat by keeping the cat indoors, fitting it with a collar and bell, and having the cat declawed. The future of our urban lizard populations is dependent on better management of domestic cats.

western whiptail

BACKYARD REPTILES

Arizona Mountain Kingsnake
Lampropeltis pyromelana

Characteristics:
A medium-sized, semi-slender snake; ringed with variable red, white and black bands; snout white or pale yellow.

This strikingly beautiful snake lives in the chaparral, pinyon/juniper woodlands and ponderosa pine forests of the central Arizona uplands. It is also fond of the lush vegetation of riparian areas. A subspecies of the Sonoran moun-

tain kingsnake, the Arizona mountain kingsnake lives among thick clumps of brush, rock outcrops, granite boulders and under fallen logs.

Mountain kingsnakes prey on birds, small mammals, lizards and other snakes. They kill their prey by constriction before eating it. The title "kingsnake" refers to their predation on other snakes. Kingsnakes are immune to rattlesnake venom and are known for their ability to kill rattlers. For this reason, they should be considered a welcome member of your backyard wildlife community.

Because of their beautiful coloration, mountain kingsnakes are prized pets for snake collectors. Unfortunately, unethical collection methods often destroy rock crevices and fallen wood where kingsnakes live. This has had a severe impact on some local kingsnake populations. Like all wild creatures, kingsnakes are better off in the wild, and their capture is strictly regulated by the Arizona Game and Fish Department.

The Arizona mountain kingsnake is sometimes confused with the venomous western coral snake (*Micruroides euryxanthus*), which is a very uncommon resident in the central Arizona uplands. They can be differentiated from kingsnakes by the pattern of wide, red bands bordered by yellow bands and by having a black snout. The Arizona mountain kingsnake has black bordering its red bands and a white or light-yellow snout.

Garter Snake
Thamnophis spp.

Characteristics:
Slender, small, greenish-brown snakes; head slightly wider than neck; most with three pale-yellow or orange lengthwise stripes.

All of the garter snakes in the central Arizona uplands are aquatic or semi-aquatic, and therefore live in riparian areas. Our most common garter snakes include the wandering (*T. elegans vagrans*), the black-necked (*T. cyrtopsis*) and the narrow-headed (*T. rufipunctatus*). The name garter snake came from the resemblance of the snake's stripes

to an old fashioned garter used to hold up a woman's stockings.

Garter snakes eat frogs, toads, tadpoles, crustaceans, fish, lizards and invertebrates. They are, in turn, the prey of ravens, hawks, raccoons, skunks and ringtails. Many garter snakes fall prey to bullfrogs (*Rana catesbeiana*). This non-native species of frog is a ravenous predator and has had a serious impact on Mexican garter snake (*T. eques*) populations, as well as on native frogs and fish.

Females of a number of garter-snake species are capable of storing sperm for fertilizing an egg which they have not yet produced. Encounters between male and female garter snakes are infrequent, and their reproductive cycles may not be synchronized when they do meet. This adaptation, called delayed fertilization, allows the female snake to produce her next litter without waiting for another encounter with a male snake. Most garter snakes bear between five and twenty-five young during the summer months. The young are nourished in their mother's womb and are born live, rather than hatching from eggs, as many snakes do.

BACKYARD REPTILES

Arizona Black Rattlesnake
Crotalus viridis cerberus

Characteristics:
A medium-sized rattlesnake of 2 to 3 feet in length; gray, brown or black blocks are separated by light, yellowish lines; sometimes solid black.

The Arizona black is the most common rattlesnake in the central Arizona uplands. It lives in the chaparral, pinyon/juniper woodland and ponderosa pine forests. Locally

known as the "timber rattler," this snake is one of the eleven subspecies of the western rattlesnake.

Active during both day and night, Arizona black rattlesnakes are often seen at springs or around other water sources. Here they lie in wait for a mouse, small bird, lizard or frog to come to drink, then they seize it as prey. Rattlesnakes have very poor eyesight and can see clearly only up to fifteen feet. They make up for this with a keen sense of smell and a specially evolved heat-sensing pit located just below the nostril. This heat-sensing ability makes them swift and efficient predators of warm-blooded animals such as mice and birds.

As a rattlesnake grows, it adds segments to its rattle. Each time it sheds its skin (usually twice a year), it gains another segment. Some individuals shed their skin only once a year, but others shed it up to four times a year. The number of segments on a snake's rattle is not directly equivalent to age, but to the number of times that it has shed its skin.

The coloration of the Arizona black varies from a medium brown to jet black. Like all pit vipers, it has a wide, spade-shaped head, and vertical, slit-like pupils. Contrary to popular belief, Arizona blacks, like all rattlesnakes, are not aggressive, and usually avoid people. The horrible stories of rattlesnakes leaping out and chasing people are tall tales exaggerated by fear. The first defense of a rattlesnake is usually an attempt to slither off unnoticed. If you get too close, or if the snake feels threatened, it will sound its rattle as a warning and to alert you to its presence. Rattling is a defensive action and should be viewed as the snake's way of saying, "Don't bother me. I'm dangerous and I will defend myself if necessary." Rattling doesn't mean that a snake is about to attack, but heed its warning before it assumes the aggressive posture of coiling and raising its head.

Getting bitten by a rattlesnake is very unlikely. To put

the chance of being bitten by a rattlesnake into perspective, it is 200 times more probable that you will be struck by lightning than that you will be bitten by a rattlesnake in your lifetime. Most bites do not result in death. The majority of those who do die after a bite are young children.

Most snakebites occur when people are turning over rocks, collecting firewood or reaching into holes or crevices. To avoid the danger of snakebite, watch where you put your hands and feet, don't reach or step into places without looking, and don't put your hands or feet into places you cannot see.

The best way to prevent rattlesnakes from living near your home is to limit their food and cover. Most rattlesnakes feed largely on rodents and other small mammals. Rodent populations can be controlled by filling in burrows, by cutting thickets of weeds and grasses, and by trapping them. Rattlesnakes are secretive and like to hide under boards, in brush piles and in other refuse. Don't allow this type of shelter to accumulate on your property. A rattlesnake-proof fence can be constructed by placing sheet metal along the lower two feet of a conventional wooden or chain-link fence, thus eliminating any climbing holds. Gates must have a tight fit or a weather-stripping barrier. Also, reducing threats to other harmless snakes will keep rattlers away. Many of these harmless snakes are competitors with rattlesnakes for food, and some of them, such as the common kingsnake, will actually kill rattlesnakes.

If you have a problem with a rattlesnake, it is best to leave trapping, eradication, or removal of it to a professional. Trying to remove a snake from your property is an aggressive action, and a rattlesnake will defend itself with all of its venomous capabilities. If there is a rattlesnake around your house, it is probably just passing through from some other place and represents only a short-term threat. In this case, you can simply avoid the snake until it leaves.

If it persists, contact your local animal-control office. They may have personnel trained to capture rattlesnakes. If animal control is unable to respond to your problem, call the nearest Arizona Game and Fish regional office. They will either send out a local wildlife manager or recommend a licensed wildlife-service company in your area.

Rattlesnakes play an important role in controlling rodent populations and are part of the natural ecological system. Many people will kill rattlesnakes out of fear and ignorance, but there are very few circumstances where killing a snake is necessary. Many nonvenomous snakes have similar markings, shake their tails and try to intimidate predators by imitating rattlesnakes. This can lead to confusion, and as a result some nonvenomous and beneficial snake species are killed. Killing a rattlesnake requires a valid Arizona hunting license, and several rattlesnakes are imperiled species that are protected by law. Contact a professional before you take any action toward the removal or elimination of a rattlesnake.

Appendix A

HELPFUL ORGANIZATIONS AND AGENCIES

- Arizona Game and Fish Department
    Region II (Flagstaff, Sedona, Williams)
        3500 S. Lake Mary Road,
        Flagstaff, AZ 86001
        (520) 774-5045
    Region III (Prescott, Cottonwood, Camp Verde)
        5325 N. Stockton Hill Road,
        Kingman, AZ 86401
        (520) 692-7700
    Region VI (Payson)
        7200 E. University,
        Mesa, AZ 85207
        (602) 981-9400
- Bat Conservation International
    P.O. Box 162603, Austin, TX 78716
    (512) 327-9721
- City Animal Control
    Camp Verde Police Dept. (520) 567-6621
    Cottonwood Police Dept. (520) 634-4246
    Flagstaff Police Dept. (520) 774-1414
    Payson Police Dept. (520)474-5177
    Prescott Police Dept. (520) 771-7701
    Prescott Valley Animal Control (520) 772-9261
    Sedona Police Dept. (520) 282-3100
- Coconino County Animal Control
    (520) 779-5164

- Coconino National Forest
    2323 E. Greenlaw Lane, Flagstaff, AZ 86004-1890
    (520) 527-3600
- The Humane Society of the United States
    2100 L Street NW, Washington, D.C. 20037
    (202) 452-1100
- Kaibab National Forest
    800 S. 6th Street, Williams, AZ 86046
    (520) 635-2681
- National Institute for Urban Wildlife
    P.O. Box 3015, Shepardstown, WV 25443
    (304) 876-6146
- National Wildlife Federation
    1400 16th Street, Washington, D.C. 20036-2266
    (202) 797-6800
- Northern Arizona Audubon Society
    P.O. Box 1496, Sedona, AZ 86339
- Prescott Audubon Society
    P.O. Box 4156, Prescott, AZ 86302
- Prescott National Forest
    230 S. Cortez, Prescott, AZ 86301
    (520) 445-1762
- Sharlot Hall Museum
    415 W. Gurley, Prescott, AZ 86301
    (520) 445-3122
- University of Arizona Cooperative Agricultural Extension-Coconino County
    2400 Huffer, Flagstaff, AZ 86001
    (520) 774-1868
- University of Arizona Cooperative Agricultural Extension-Yavapai County
    500 S. Marina, Prescott, AZ 86301
    (520) 445-6590
- Yavapai County Animal Control, Sherrif's Department
    (520) 771-3260

Appendix B

FURTHER READING

Buff, Sheila. *The Birdfeeder's Handbook.* New York, New York: Lyons and Burford, Publishers, 1991.

Burton, Robert. *The National Audubon Society North American Birdfeeder Handbook.* New York, New York: Dorling Kindersley, Inc., 1992.

California Center for Wildlife. *Living With Wildlife: How to Enjoy, Cope With, and Protect North America's Wild Creatures Around Your Home and Theirs.* San Francisco, California. 1994.

Day, Gerald I. *Javelina Research and Management in Arizona.* Phoenix, Arizona: Arizona Game and Fish Department.

Ehrlich, Paul R., David S. Dobkin, and Darryl Wheye. *The Birder's Handbook: A Field Guide to the Natural History of North American Birds.* New York, New York: Simon and Schuster, 1988.

Ernst, Ruth Shaw. *The Naturalist's Garden.* Emmaus, Pennsylvania: Rodale Press, 1987.

Harrison, George H. *The Backyard Bird Watcher.* New York, New York: Simon and Schuster, 1979.

Harrison, George and Kit. *America's Favorite Backyard Wildlife.* New York, New York: Simon and Schuster, 1985.

Hodge, Guy R. (Ed.). *Pocket Guide to the Humane Control of Wildlife in Cities and Towns.* Helena, Montana: The Humane Society of the United States and Falcon Press, 1991.

Hoffmeister, Donald F. *Mammals of Arizona.* Tucson, Arizona: The University of Arizona Press and The Arizona Game and Fish Department, 1986.

Johnsgard, Paul A. *The Hummingbirds of North America.* Washington, D.C.: Smithsonian Institution, 1983.

Leedy, Daniel L., and Lowell W. Adams. *A Guide to Urban Wildlife Management.* Columbia, Maryland: National Institute for Urban Wildlife, 1984.

Lowe, Charles H., Cecil R. Schwalbe and Terry B. Johnson. *The Venomous Reptiles of Arizona.* Phoenix, Arizona: Arizona Game and Fish Department, 1986.

Merilees, Bill. *Attracting Backyard Wildlife.* Altona, Manitoba, Canada: Friesen printers, 1989.

Peterson, Roger Tory. *A Field Guide to Western Birds.* Boston, Massachusetts: Houghton Mifflin Company, 1990

Shaw, Charles E. and Sheldon Campbell. *Snakes of the American West.* New York: Alfred A. Knopf, Inc., 1974.

Terres, John K. *The Audubon Society Encyclopedia of North American Birds.* New York: Alfred A. Knopf, Inc., 1980.

Tuttle, Merlin D. *America's Neighborhood Bats.* Austin, Texas: University of Texas Press, 1988.

Stebbins, Robert C. *A Field Guide to Western Reptiles and Amphibians.* New York, New York: Houghton Mifflin Company, 1985.

About the Author

ROBERT HOFFA is a teacher, writer, and researcher whose lifelong love of nature has led him to work in Yellowstone, Grand Canyon, and Everglades National Parks, as well as to hike the Applachian Trail. He has worked as an interpreter for the National Park Service, as a teacher and coordinator of wilderness trips, and in a variety of inventory, monitoring and field biology jobs on public lands. For the past four years, he has worked for the Prescott National Forest. Bob holds a Bachelor of Arts in Natural History and Outdoor Education. He works in Central Arizona, living out his passion for learning from the wisdom of the Earth.

About the Illustrator

WALT ANDERSON considers himself an interpreter of the natural world, a broad goal that allows him to "interpret" through drawing and painting, photography, guiding expeditions around the world, and teaching at the innovative Prescott College. His next major project will be writing and illustrating (drawings and photographs) a book entitled *Sky Islands of the American Southwest: A Natural History.*